Anonymous

Spanish Rule in Cuba

Laws governing the Island

Anonymous

Spanish Rule in Cuba
Laws governing the Island

ISBN/EAN: 9783337154332

Printed in Europe, USA, Canada, Australia, Japan

Cover: Foto ©ninafisch / pixelio.de

More available books at **www.hansebooks.com**

SPANISH RULE IN CUBA.

LAWS GOVERNING THE ISLAND.

REVIEW PUBLISHED BY THE COLONIAL OFFICE IN MADRID, WITH DATA AND STATISTICS COMPILED FROM OFFICIAL RECORDS.

(AUTHORIZED TRANSLATION, WITH ADDITIONAL NOTES.)

NEW YORK:

1896.

INTRODUCTION.

WHEN accusations are based upon falsehood and misrepresentation truth should demand its rights and enforce the respect which is its due.

So many calumnies have been hurled at Spain by those who are interested in the Cuban revolt, and by their sympathizers, that their refutation has become a duty. To perform this duty is the object of these pages.

They contain a sketch of the laws under which the island of Cuba is governed. The dates of all the laws are given and the text of the more important acts is given in full.

The laws of Cuba show that the legislation of the island has kept pace with that of the most advanced nations. They prove that the judicial institutions of Cuba are equal to those of the most enlightened countries, and that the liberties of her inhabitants rival those of the citizens of the most democratic nations.

Cuba long ago ceased to be a colony. She is now an integral part of Spain. All Spaniards, be they born in the Peninsula or in Cuba, may say: "Where Spain has her flag, there is Spain."

INDEX.

		PAGE
	INTRODUCTION,	7
I.	LAWS OF THE INDIES—THEIR CHANGES—UNWARRANTED REVOLTS,	9
II.	THE ZANJON CAPITULATION—ALL DEMANDS CONCEDED,	11
III.	ABOLITION OF SLAVERY—ABOLITION LAW,	13
IV.	POLITICAL ORGANIZATION—THE CONSTITUTION OF SPAIN EXTENDED TO CUBA—AMPLE LIBERTIES AND REPRESENTATION ACCORDED,	18
V.	ELECTORAL LAW—SENATORS AND REPRESENTATIVES TO THE CORTES,	20
VI.	PUBLIC MEETINGS AND ASSOCIATIONS,	24
VII.	THE GOVERNOR-GENERAL—HIS POWERS AND DUTIES DEFINED,	25
VIII.	PROVINCIAL ADMINISTRATION,	28
IX.	MUNICIPAL ADMINISTRATION,	28
X.	PUBLIC PEACE,	29
XI.	DEPARTMENT OF JUSTICE,	30
XII.	CIVIL RIGHTS,	30
XIII.	THE LAW MERCHANT,	32
XIV.	MORTGAGES,	33
XV.	REGISTRY AND CIVIL MARRIAGE,	33
XVI.	NOTARIES,	34
XVII.	CRIMINAL LAW,	35
XVIII.	PUBLIC INSTRUCTION,	36
XIX.	ECONOMICS—TAX REDUCTION,	37
XX.	CUBA'S PUBLIC DEBT—ITS ORIGIN,	41
XXI.	APPOINTMENTS TO PUBLIC OFFICE—CUBANS IN HIGH AND MINOR OFFICES BOTH IN CUBA AND IN THE GOVERNMENT OF SPAIN,	41
XXII.	UNIFICATION OF STATE PROFESSIONS IN THE PENINSULA AND IN THE COLONIAL PROVINCES,	47
XXIII.	REMARKS—THE AUTONOMIST MANIFESTO,	48
XXIV.	REFORM LAW OF 1895, FOR CUBA AND PORTO RICO,	51
XXV.	CONCLUSION,	66
	APPENDIX—STATISTICS,	i-v.

I.

LAWS OF THE INDIES.*

Their Changes—Unwarranted Revolts.

SPAIN has ever proved her eagerness to favor the interests and well-being of her transatlantic possessions. The discoverer of a world, in the pride of her achievement she toiled with a mother's tenderness to surround her children with all manner of guarantees of prosperity and development. The Spanish legislation for the Indies is a monument to the rectitude and foresight with which the metropolis sought the growth of her colonies through the moderation and justice of her policy toward the inhabitants of the conquered lands. *[Policy of Moderation and Justice.]*

Under these wise laws the first and essential duties of a grantee of land toward the inhabitants of his grant was to train the natives in good morals, to teach them the Christian faith, preaching it to them for their salvation, and to treat, aid and defend them as he would treat, aid and defend the other Spanish subjects and vassals : so that by such beneficent means the natives might be drawn toward the suzerainty of Spain. These laws were intended for the good and for the preservation of the natives, and sought to close every channel through which injury might reach them. For the indoctrination and protection of the natives and of the slaves, negroes and mulattoes, priests were appointed and parishes established throughout the Indies ; for them schools and hospitals were founded and endowed ; their punishment with fines was prohibited ; their lawsuits were ordered to be speedily tried ; the Indians were forbidden to sell their daughters, even in marriage ; such native usages and customs as were subservient to good government were ordered to be respected ; the laws intended for the benefit of the natives were ordered to be put into immediate effect, without prejudice to the right of appeal, while in many other provisions the law guaranteed the personal liberty of the Indians, the possession and enjoyment of their property, and provided remedies for damages and safeguards against injury. *[First Steps Toward Civilization.]*

Such was the first code of Spain for her dominions beyond the seas.

The laws of the Indies, however, intended for a primitive epoch of calm and peace, of simplicity of life, of commercial isolation and

---
* The Spanish possessions in America were termed the Indies.

of local exclusiveness, had to give way to reforms adequate to the legitimate aspirations of the colonists, whose advancing education and whose large and profitable trade imposed the necessity of converting the colonies into Spanish provinces, similar in organization, rights and duties to the other provinces of the kingdom. And that has gradually been done since the middle of the present century.

Cuban Revolts Coincident with Liberal Reforms.

But it is noteworthy that the outbreaks of Cuban insurrections have coincided in time with the intentions of the metropolis to transplant to Cuba the most radical legislative innovations, which innovations have been deemed in Spain marks of progress. The Cuban revolt of Yara* was almost simultaneous with the Spanish democratic revolution of 1868.† In spite of the democratic ideas which bred that revolution in Spain the Cuban separatist struggle lasted ten years. And although during that critical period Spain was discouraged and ruined by the efforts required for other civil wars at home, those ten years were insufficient to exhaust her energy, the separatist struggle finally terminating in an absolute pardon for the rebels and large and advantageous concessions to Cuba. The actual revolt began also at the very moment when the Chambers at Madrid were giving their attention in a liberal spirit to the solution of colonial problems.

Spain's Promises Fulfilled.

How can the singular behavior of those who rise in arms to break every bond of union with the mother country be justified? No reason can explain it; no pretext may excuse it. Spain has discharged all the duties of a metropolis mindful of the interests of her colonies, and has kept every promise of the Zanjon capitulation.‡ To prove the former it is sufficient to glance at the Cuban political and administrative situation, adapted progressively to the advances introduced into the national legislation. To believe the latter no testimony is necessary save that of the facts themselves, which facts are in harmony with the demands of the Cuban capitulants of 1878.

Reform Legislation.

Slavery has been totally abolished; the Cubans have been granted the same rights as other Spaniards; they are represented in the Cortes; their provincial and municipal administration is surrounded by guarantees; the civil and criminal laws of Spain, administered by tribunals similar to those of the Peninsula, have been established in Cuba; public instruction has been organized upon the same basis as in Spain; the economic legislation for Cuba has been regulated to facilitate the prosperity and wealth of that magnificent portion of America; and if aught were lacking in

* A small town in the province of Santiago de Cuba. There the revolt of 1868-78 began.

† The revolution which drove Isabel II. from the throne.

‡ The Cuban revolt which began in 1868 ended with the capitulation, which took place at the Zanjon in 1878. Vide Chapter II., page 11.

an administration and a government entirely free from restrictions and drawbacks, local or regional, the law of March 15, 1895, has blotted away all suspicion of selfishness on the part of the mother country.

II.

THE ZANJON CAPITULATION.

Articles of Capitulation.

"The people and the armed forces of the Central Department,* and armed groups from other departments, having met in convention as the only fit means of terminating, in one sense or another, the pending negotiations, and having considered the propositions submitted by the commander-in-chief of the Spanish army, determined on their part to propose amendments to said propositions by presenting the following Articles of Capitulation:

ARTICLE I. The political, organic and administrative laws enjoyed by Porto Rico shall be established in Cuba.

ART. II. Free pardon for all political offenses committed from 1868 to date, and freedom for those who are under indictment or are serving sentences within or without the island. Amnesty to all deserters from the Spanish army, regardless of nationality, this clause being extended to include all those who have taken part directly or indirectly in the revolutionary movement.

ART. III. Freedom for the Asiatic coolies† and for the slaves who may be in the insurgent ranks.

ART. IV. No individual who by virtue of this capitulation shall submit to and remain under the authority of the Spanish Government shall be compelled to render any military service before peace be established over the whole territory.

ART. V. Every individual who by virtue of this capitulation may wish to depart from the island shall be permitted to do so, and the Spanish Government shall provide him with the means therefor, without passing through any town or settlement, if he so desire.

ART. VI. The capitulation of each force shall take place in uninhabited spots, where beforehand the arms and other munitions of war shall be deposited.

ART. VII. In order to further the acceptation, by the insurgents of the other departments, of these Articles of Capitulation, the commander-in-chief of the Spanish army shall furnish them free transportation, by land and sea, over all the lines within his control, to the Central Department.

ART. VIII. This pact with the committee of the Central De-

---

*The Central Department was one of the three military districts of the island, and was composed of the present provinces of Puerto Principe and Santa Clara. The main force of the rebels was in this department.

†These coolies were Chinese who had been imported under contract to serve for a term of eight years, and who had broken their contracts.

partment shall be deemed to have been made with all the departments of the island which may accept its conditions.

ENCAMPMENT OF ST. AGUSTIN, February 10, 1878.

E. L. LUACES.

RAFAEL RODRIGUEZ, Secretary.

Demands of the Insurgents.

This document includes:

The political and administrative organization of Cuba.

Pardon of political offenses, freedom of persons under indictment, and amnesty for deserters.

The emancipation of the coolies and the slaves within the rebel ranks.

Free transportation for those desirous of leaving the island.

Exemption of the capitulants from military service until the whole territory of the island was pacified.

Treatment of the Capitulants.

No complaints were heard of the lack of frankness, nay of cordiality, in the reception of the capitulants after their surrender. All dissension between those who again became brethren ceased. When the arms had been laid down, the commander-in chief and the Spanish Government gladly sought to tighten those bonds of mutual affection, esteem and sympathy which were to throw wide open before the insurgents the doors of the nation, and make them sharers of the national life equally with other citizens of Spain. Some of the capitulants, men noted during the war, went to Madrid, and, far from being received in official circles with prejudice and suspicion, obtained government offices, and a means of subsistence derived from the revenues of the state, or under the patronage of men eminent in the politics of the nation took positions in banks and mercantile firms, or practiced the arts or established industries.*

The facts will readily bear witness to the manner in which the other articles of the capitulation were kept.

In fact, the new organization of the island of Cuba, which was to be like that of Porto Rico, has been established in so generous and benevolent a spirit that to-day the natives of the latter island complain because the franchise is more restricted in Porto Rico than in Cuba. In this respect, as in all others, the mother country has more than kept the pledges of the Zanjon treaty.

* Among the Cubans who took part in the former war and who actually continue filling, to the satisfaction of the administration, government offices in Spain are the following: Señores Martinez, Freire, Fonseca, Roa, Ramirez and Figueredo. Calixto Garcia had a position in the Banco Hipotecario. The rebel chieftain Lacret, who, like the former, seems to have disregarded the promises he made and the favors he received, was for a long time in business in the mother country.

III.

ABOLITION OF SLAVERY.

From the time of the Zanjon treaty, through the measures which secured the inhabitants of the possessions of Spain in the Antilles in their rights as citizens, regardless of race or color, slavery disappeared from Spanish America.

<small>Slavery Totally Abolished.</small>

According to Art. 3 of the Articles of Capitulation only the coolies and slaves who were in the rebel ranks were to be freed. Spain, however, made a more ample and generous concession. The decree of October 15, 1868, emancipated the children born of slave mothers after September 17 of that year. The act of July 4, 1870, emancipated the children born after that date, the slaves who had served under the Spanish flag, those who had reached the age of sixty years, and those which belonged to the state. The act of February 13, 1880, abolished the state of slavery, and provided that the slaves included in the census of 1871 should remain under the apprenticeship* of their possessors for a term lasting from five to eight years, according to the number and ages of the apprenticed laborers of each employer. But the term of eight years had not expired when the Spanish Government, anticipating the law, declared, by the royal decree of October 17, 1886, that from the time of the proclamation of that decree in Cuba the system of apprenticeship established in 1880 should cease, and obliterated for ever all vestiges of slavery in the Spanish dominions. Thus Spain conceded far more than had been demanded by the capitulants of 1878.

ABOLITION LAW.

ACT OF FEBRUARY 13, 1880.

Alfonso XII., by the grace of God Constitutional King of Spain.

To all whom these presents shall come, know ye: that the Cortes have decreed and we sanctioned the following:

ARTICLE I. Slavery in the island of Cuba shall cease, in accordance with this law.

---

*Chap. 73 of 3 and 4 Will. IV. abolished slavery in the British West Indies by substituting for the relation of "master and slave" the relation of "employer and apprenticed labourer," which was to cease at the end of a fixed period. The Spanish act is similar to the English statute. The term used in the Spanish act is *patronato*, from the Latin *patronatus*, the relation existing between patron and client. In Rome emancipation did not confer, as a rule, absolute freedom. The emancipated slave, the freedman (*i. e.*, freed man), became the client of his former master, and was termed *libertus*. This is the term applied by the Spanish statute to former slaves emancipated under previous laws and who were not yet in full possession of their civil rights. The "apprenticed labourers" of the English statute and the "patrocinados" of the Spanish act correspond rather to the "statu liberi" of Rome.

Employer May Alienate His Rights Over His Apprenticed Laborers, but Members of a Family Must Not Be Separated.

ART. II. The persons who were registered as slaves in the census of 1871, without violation of the act of July 4, 1870, and who still continue in slavery at the time of proclamation of this act, shall remain during the period herein fixed as the apprenticed laborers of their possessors.

The right of an employer to the services of his apprenticed laborer shall be alienable by all the means known to the law. But no employer shall alienate his right to the services of a child under twelve years of age without alienating his right to the services of the child's father and mother to the new employer. If he alienate his right to the services of a parent, he must also alienate his right to the services of the children under twelve years of age to the new employer. In no case shall the members of a family group be separated.

Rights and Duties of Employers.

ART. III. The employer shall preserve his right to utilize the services of his apprenticed laborer, and to be his legal representative.

ART. IV. The duties of the employer are :
1. To feed his apprenticed laborers.
2. To clothe them.
3. To attend to them when ill.
4. To compensate them for their services with the stipend herein fixed.
5. To give minors a common-school education and the training necessary to practice some useful art or trade.
6. To feed and clothe his apprenticed laborers' children, infants, and non-adults, born before and after the apprenticeship, and attend to them when ill, the employer being permitted to avail himself of the services of such children without compensation.

ART. V. Upon the proclamation of this act every apprenticed laborer shall be given a written notice, in the form the regulations shall prescribe, informing him of the substance of the rights and duties of his new state.

Wages of Apprenticed Laborers.

ART. VI. The monthly stipend referred to in Sec. 4 of Art. IV. shall be from one to two dollars for those between eighteen years of age and the age of majority,* and three dollars for those who have attained their majority.

In case of incapacity to labor, owing to illness, or to any other cause, the employer shall be exempt from payment of the stipend corresponding to the time such incapacity may last.

ART. VII. The apprenticeship shall terminate :
1. By extinction, under a classification of the apprenticed laborers according to seniority, in the manner specified by Art. VIII, so that the apprenticeship shall cease absolutely at the end of eight years from the time of proclamation of this act.
2. By mutual agreement between the employer and the apprenticed laborer, without the intervention of a third party. But if the apprenticed laborer be under twenty years of age his parents, if known, may intervene, or, in their default, the local board may interpose, the age of the apprenticed laborer being determined as provided in Art. XIII.
3. At the option of the employer, unless the apprenticed laborer be a minor or a sexagenarian, or be ill or disabled.

* *I. e., twenty-five years.*

4. By indemnification to the master for the loss of his apprenticed laborer's services. The indemnification shall be of from thirty to fifty dollars a year, according to the age, sex and condition of the apprenticed laborer, for each year still unserved of the first five years, and the same amount a year for half of what part of the final three years he may be required to serve.*

5. Through any cause of emancipation provided by the civil and penal laws, or through the failure of the employer to discharge the duties imposed upon him by Art. IV.

ART. VIII. The extinction of the apprenticeship under the classification, according to seniority, referred to in Sec. 1 of Art. VII., shall take place by fourth parts of the number of apprenticed laborers subject to each employer, commencing at the end of the fifth year, and continuing at the end of each successive year, until at the end of the eighth year the institution shall cease absolutely. Provisions for the Extinction of this Institution.

The selection of the apprenticed laborers according to seniority shall be made before the local board a month before the end of the fifth year and of each of the remaining years. If in any year the number of apprenticed laborers of the same age be greater than the number to be freed, the selection shall be by lot cast before the board.

If the number of apprenticed laborers be greater than four, and be not divisible by four, the excess shall be distributed among the first three classes, beginning with the first.

If the number of apprenticed laborers be under four, the selection shall be by thirds, by halves, or singly; but the employer shall not be under obligation to discharge his apprenticed laborers until the end of the sixth, the seventh, or the eighth year respectively.†

The regulations shall fix the method of making the registers and taking the census necessary to the selections.

ART. IX. Those who have been discharged from their apprenticeship, in accordance with Art. VII., shall be granted civil rights, but they shall continue under the protection of the state and subject to laws and regulations which shall require them to prove that they are under contract to labor,‡ or are occupied in some trade or useful occupation. To Prevent Vagrancy.

Orphans under twenty years of age shall be under the tutelage of the state.

ART. X. The obligation by those who have been discharged from apprenticeship to prove a contract to labor shall last four years. Those who disregard this obligation shall, at the discretion of the mayor, upon the advice of the local board, be deemed guilty of vagrancy and may be condemned to labor for pay on public works for a term fixed by the regulations for the particular case. At the end of the four years referred to in this article those who have been freed from apprenticeship shall have full civil and political rights.

---

* Under the classification of Art. VIII. an apprenticed laborer might not be bound to serve the whole of the final three years.

† *I. e.*, an employer of but one apprenticed laborer would not be required to discharge him before the end of the eighth year; an employer of two would discharge one at the end of the seventh year and the other at the end of the eighth year; an employer of three would discharge one at the end of the sixth year, &c.

‡ This was to prevent vagrancy, the proof of being under contract to labor meaning simply proof of being in employment.

Art. XI. Those who previous to the promulgation of this act have bargained for their freedom with their possessors shall retain the rights acquired by their bargain. They may, in addition, take advantage of Sec. 4, Art. VII., by paying their employers the difference between the sum due under the said Sec. 4, Art. VII., and the sum already paid.

Art. XII. Those who by virtue of the act of July 4, 1870, are free, through having been born after September 17, 1868, shall be subject to the provisions of that act, except in so far as this law may be more advantageous to them.

Freedmen,* emancipated under Art. XIX. of the said act of 1870, shall continue under the tutelage of the state, and shall for four years be obliged to prove the existence of their contracts to labor and fulfill the other requirements as to occupation, referred to in Arts. IX. and X. hereof.

Art. XIII. For the purposes of this act the term "minor" shall be understood to refer to a child under seven. If the age be unknown the local boards shall determine the age, taking into consideration the physical appearance of the minor and the advice of an expert.

Corporal Punishment Prohibited.

Art. XIV. Employers shall not, even under pretext of maintaining the good order and discipline of the work on their plantations, inflict corporal punishment on their apprenticed laborers, as prohibited by Sec. 2, Art. XXIX. of the act of July 4, 1870. They shall, however, have the coercitive and disciplinary rights provided by the regulations, which shall contain rules both to secure the attendance of apprenticed laborers at their work and to prevent the exaction of excessive labor.

Employers may also reduce the monthly stipend of an apprenticed laborer by an amount proportionate to the absence from his labor, in the cases and in the manner determined by the regulations.

Local Boards Created to Enforce this Act.

Art. XV. A board presided over by the Provincial Governor, and, in his absence, by the president of the Provincial Assembly, shall be organized in each province. The board shall consist of a provincial assemblyman, the judge of the district court, the district attorney, the corporation counsel of the provincial capital and two taxpayers, one of whom must be an employer of apprenticed laborers.

Local boards, in the discretion of the respective provincial governors and upon the previous approbation of the Governor-General, shall be organized in the municipalities where convenient. Each board shall be presided over by the mayor, and shall consist of the corporation counsel, a principal taxpayer, and two reputable citizens. These boards and the district attorney shall attend to the rigid enforcement of this act, and shall have, in addition to the powers specified herein, the powers entrusted to them by the regulations.

Art. XVI. Apprenticed laborers shall be subject to the jurisdiction of the ordinary courts for their misdemeanors and crimes, under the Penal Code, but for rebellion, sedition and rioting they shall be tried by military tribunals.

Nevertheless, when apprenticed laborers disturb the good order and discipline of the work, employers, if their disciplinary powers

---

* For "freedman" see note page 13.

be insufficient, may call upon the Governor-General for aid against their apprenticed laborers. At the third justifiable complaint the apprenticed laborer may be sentenced to serve in the public works for the term fixed, according to the offense, by the regulations, and not exceeding the amount of time remaining before his discharge from apprenticeship. If, while serving his sentence, the apprenticed laborer should be guilty of a serious breach of discipline or should abandon his work, or if after serving his sentence he should again be guilty of his previous offense, the Governor-General may, upon information with specific reasons to the Supreme Government, order the apprenticed laborer to be transported to the Spanish islands on the African coast, where he shall remain subject to the supervision fixed by the regulations. _{Penalties for Refractory Apprenticed Laborers.}

ART. XVII. The regulations to which this act refers shall be made within a term of sixty days from the receipt of a copy of this act by the Governor-General, after consulting the Archbishop of Santiago, the Bishop of Havana, the Supreme Court of Havana, and the Council of Administration. At the end of said term, which shall not be extensible, he shall proclaim and enforce the act and the regulations. He must send to the Supreme Government by the first mail a copy of the regulations for approval, and the Supreme Government, after hearing the Council of State, shall signify its approval or disapproval of the regulations within a month from the receipt of said copy. _{Framing of Regulations.}

ART. XVIII. All laws, regulations and ordinances inconsistent with this act, with the exception of such of their provisions as may be modified by the foregoing articles, are hereby annulled, without prejudice of the rights acquired by slaves and freedmen under the act of July 4, 1870.

Therefore, we command all the courts, justices, heads of departments, governors and other authorities, civil, military and ecclesiastical, of whatsoever class and degree, to keep, and cause to be kept, enforce and execute this law in all its parts.

Given in the Palace, February 13, 1880.

I, THE KING.

The Minister of the Colonies,

JOSÉ ELDUAYEN.

ABOLITION OF APPRENTICESHIP TO LABOR.

Royal Decree of October 7, 1886.

Upon the proposition of the Minister of the Colonies and with the concurrence of the Council of Ministers, in the name of my august son, King Alfonso XIII., and as Queen Regent of the kingdom, I decree as follows:

ARTICLE I. From the proclamation of this decree in the island of Cuba the apprenticeship to labor established by the act of February 13, 1880, shall cease.

ART. II. The apprenticed laborers now existing shall continue in the state of those referred to in Art. VII. of said act,* and subject, therefore, to the provisions of Arts. IX. and X. of the same.

ART. III. The authorities shall take scrupulous care that the provisions of Chapter IV. of the regulations of May 8, 1880, be

---

* See p. 14.

enforced, and that without loss of time the new freedmen be provided with the certificate referred to in Art. LXXXIII. of said regulations.

ART. IV. Apart from the duties imposed upon Government officials by Art. LXXIII. of the regulations of May 8, these officials shall see that the apprenticed laborers who have been discharged from apprenticeship, and who have not completed the term of four years referred to in Art. X. of the aforesaid act, shall present every three months to the mayors of the municipalities within which they reside their freedmen's certificates and some document proving that they are under contract to labor.

The mayors of the municipalities shall keep a register of those who shall have presented themselves, and shall place the delinquents at the disposal of the superior authorities of the province, who shall comply with the provisions of Art. X.* of the act of February 13, and the corresponding articles of the regulations of May 8.

ART. V. The provincial and local boards created by Art. XV.† of the act of February 13 are hereby suppressed, and the provisions of that act which are contrary to the provisions of the present decree are hereby annulled.

Given at the Palace on October 7, 1886.

MARIA CHRISTINA.

The Minister of the Colonies,

GERMAN GAMAZO.

IV.

POLITICAL ORGANIZATION.

The Constitution of Spain Extended to Cuba.

The Constitution of Spain, of July 2, 1876, was proclaimed in the island of Cuba by the royal decree of April 7, 1881. From that date the inhabitants of Cuba have enjoyed all the rights of Spanish citizens.

Under the Constitution no inhabitant of Cuba may be arrested except in the cases and in the manner prescribed by law. Within twenty-four hours of the arrest the prisoner must be discharged or surrendered to the judicial authorities; thereupon a judge having jurisdiction must, within seventy-two hours, either order the discharge of the prisoner or order his commitment to jail. Within the same limit of time the prisoner must be informed of the decision in his case. (Art. IV. of the Constitution.)

No Spaniard, and consequently no Cuban, may be committed except upon the warrant of a judge having jurisdiction. Within seventy-two hours of the commitment the prisoner must be granted a hearing, and the warrant of commitment either sustained or quashed. (Art. V.)

Any person arrested or committed without the formalities required by law, unless his case fall within the exceptions made by the Constitution and by the laws, shall be discharged upon his

* See p. 15.
† See p. 16.

own petition, or upon the petition of any Spanish subject. (Art. V.)

No one shall enter the dwelling of a Cuban without his consent except in the cases and in the manner prescribed by law. (Art. VI.)

His mail while in charge of the Post Office shall neither be opened nor withheld. (Art. VII.)

He shall not be compelled to change his dwelling or residence except upon the order of an authority competent thereto and in the cases provided by law. (Art. IX.)

The penalty of confiscation of property shall never be imposed upon him; nor may he be deprived of his private property unless by due process of law, and when the expropriation be for public use, after a previous just compensation. If there be no previous just compensation the courts shall protect his rights, and in the proper case restore him to the possession of his property.

The Roman Catholic and Apostolic religion is the religion of the state. But no Cuban shall suffer molestation on account of his religious opinions, nor be disturbed in the practice of his faith, provided he duly respect Christian morals. (Art. XI.) *Freedom of Worship.*

The learned professions are open to all Spanish subjects and they may obtain their professional instruction in any manner they deem fit. Any Spanish subject may establish and conduct a school, in accordance with the laws. (Art. XII.)

Every Cuban, like every Spaniard, has the right:

Freely to express his ideas and opinions, orally or in writing, using the printing press or any similar device, without censorship.

Peaceably to assemble.

To form associations. *Freedom of the Press and of Meeting.*

To petition, by himself or in combination with others, the King, the Cortes, and the authorities.

The right to petition is denied only to armed forces. (Art. XIII.)

All Cubans are eligible to public office, according to their merit and capacity. (Art. XV.)

The constitutional rights conceded to Cubans are guaranteed by the provisions of laws passed to enforce the Constitution. These laws provide remedies, civil and criminal, for the infringement of constitutional rights by judges, authorities and functionaries of all classes. (Art. XVI.) *Constitutional Rights Guaranteed.*

All these constitutional rights of the inhabitants of Cuba, which render their citizenship as valuable a protection as the citizenship of any other state, no matter how democratic, were secured by the organization of municipalities and provincial assemblies, and above all by representation in the Cortes, as provided by the two following articles of the Constitution:

ART. 89. The colonial provinces shall be governed by special laws; but the Government is authorized to extend to these prov-

Representation of Cuba and Porto Rico in the Spanish Cortes.
inces the laws proclaimed or that may be proclaimed for the Peninsula, with the modifications it may deem proper, informing the Cortes thereof.

Cuba and Porto Rico shall be represented in the Cortes of the kingdom, in the manner that shall be prescribed by a special law, and this law may differ for each of the islands.

PROVISIONAL ARTICLE. The Government shall determine when and in what manner the representatives of the island of Cuba to the Cortes shall be elected.

Cubans have therefore the following constitutional rights firmly established by the organic law : personal security against arbitrary arrest ; inviolability of the domicile ; security of the secrecy of correspondence ; security against confiscation of property ; the suffrage ; freedom of worship ; freedom of education, and freedom of the study and practice of professions ; freedom of speech ; freedom of the press ; right of peaceable assembly ; right to form associations ; right to petition ; eligibility to all public offices ; and a municipal and provincial government.

Is it therefore reasonable to speak of the "despotism of the mother country," or of the "irritating condition of the island of Cuba" ?

V.

ELECTORAL LAW.

SENATORS AND REPRESENTATIVES TO THE CORTES.

How Senators Are Elected.
Under the act of January 9, 1879, Cuba elects thirteen senators. Their apportionment is as follows : The province of Havana elects three senators ; the provinces of Matanzas, Pinar del Rio, Puerto Principe, Santa Clara and Santiago de Cuba two each ; the archbishopric of Santiago de Cuba one ; the University of Havana one,* and the Economic Society one.

The act of February 8, 1877, regulates the election of senators. Senators in each province are elected by secret ballot by an electoral college. This college is composed of electors chosen by the Provincial Assembly and electors chosen by secret ballot by the boards of aldermen and by the principal taxpayers.†

How Representatives Are Elected.
Representatives to the Cortes‡ are elected under the act of December 27, 1892. Their election is by popular vote, one representative for every 50,000 inhabitants. A voter must be over twenty-five years of age, a taxpayer to the amount of at least five dollars, or the possessor of a professional diploma or university

---

* Representatives of the universities of Oxford and Cambridge have seats in the House of Commons.
† Taxpayers whose taxes are above a certain amount.
‡ The Spanish Legislature is called the Cortes. It is composed of two branches : One is called the Senate, the other the Congress of Deputies.

degree. The act provides regulation for the registration of voters; for the formation of election boards; and for a secret ballot.

Cuba sends thirty representatives to the Cortes. All the formalities of elections are similar to those of the Peninsula.

The following are the clauses concerning the election of senators:

ARTICLE I. In accordance with the additional clause of the act of February 8, 1877, the provinces of Havana and Porto Rico* shall each elect three senators, and the provinces of Matanzas, Pinar del Rio, Puerto Príncipe, Santa Clara and Santiago de Cuba shall each elect two senators.

Also, and as provided therefor by law, the Archbishopric of Santiago, with its suffragans and chapters, shall elect one senator; the University of Havana, with the Institutes and Special Schools of Cuba and Porto Rico, shall elect one senator; and the Economic Societies of Cuba and Porto Rico one senator.†

The following are the provisions concerning the election of representatives to the Cortes:

ARTICLE I. The representatives to the Cortes shall be elected by popular vote. The voting shall be by sections, into which, for that purpose, the districts and circumscriptions* now established in Cuba and Porto Rico, or to be established, shall be subdivided.

Elections by Popular Vote.

After their admission to the Cortes they shall, with the representatives from the Peninsula, individually and collectively represent the nation.

ART. II. One representative at least for every 50,000 inhabitants shall be elected, and the count shall include the whole population without distinction of races.

ART. III. The Government is empowered to determine, in accordance with the results of the census of the population of Cuba and Porto Rico, the number of representatives. In the apportionment the present division into circumscriptions and districts and their subdivision into sections shall be preserved as far as possible.

Each municipality shall constitute: One section if the number of voters does not exceed 100; two sections if the number of voters does not exceed 200; three sections if the number of voters does not exceed 300, and so forth.

ART. IV. Only by special legislation will it be permissible to vary the number of representatives of Cuba and Porto Rico, or to change the boundaries of the circumscriptions, districts and sections, and the seats of the canvassing boards.

---

* The island of Porto Rico constitutes one province—the province of Porto Rico. The island of Cuba is divided into six provinces—Havana, Matanzas, Pinar del Rio, Santa Clara, Puerto Príncipe and Santiago de Cuba.

† A district elects one single representative; a circumscription elects more than one representative, each voter voting for all the representatives from his circumscription; a section is a division of the district or circumscription for convenience in casting the vote.

Who Are Eligible.

ART. V. To be eligible as representative to the Congress it is necessary:

First. To be a Spanish subject*; to be a layman†; to have reached the age of twenty-five years before the day of election; and to be in the enjoyment of all civil rights. A representative-elect who has been born a subject of Spain, and has renounced his allegiance and again recovered, as prescribed by law, his Spanish citizenship, shall prove, in order to obtain his seat as representative to the Cortes, that he recovered his Spanish citizenship at least one year before his election.

Second. To have been elected and declared elected in the Cortes as provided by this act and by the rules of the Cortes.

Third. Not to be under disability to obtain the office owing to any personal incapacity.‡

Registration Essential.

Fourth. Not to be included within any of the cases specified in the law of incompatibilities.§

ART. XII. Only those whose names shall be contained in the registration lists as voters on the day of election shall have the right to vote for representatives to the Cortes.

ART. XIII. Every male Spanish subject, resident of Cuba or of Porto Rico, shall have the right to have his name included in the registration lists of the section within which he resides, provided he be of the age of twenty-five years; he be a taxpayer, to the amount of five dollars in Cuba and ten dollars in Porto Rico, of taxes on rural or urban real estate or of industrial or commercial taxes; provided he shows he pays the said amount of taxes at the time of demanding his inscription in the registration lists. In computing the amount of his taxes only the taxes paid to the state must be considered.

To What Extent Voters Must Be Taxpayers.

ART. XIV. For the purpose of computing the amount of taxes paid by a citizen who claims the right to vote he shall be deemed a property owner in the following cases:

First. The husband shall be deemed the owner of his wife's property while the marriage exists.

Second. The father shall be deemed the owner of his child's property, if he be the legal administrator of the child's estate.

Apportionment of Taxes Among Copartners.

Third. If the legal title lie in a son, and the mother be the beneficiary, the son shall be deemed the owner.

ART. XV. For electoral purposes the copartners of a mercantile partnership shall be deemed taxpayers of the taxes paid by the partnership, the taxes being apportioned according to the interest in the partnership of each copartner. If the respective interest of each copartner be unknown the copartners shall be deemed to have an equal interest. The existence of the partnership, the interest of each copartner, and the class of each copartner shall be proved by a declaration certified by a notary and recorded in the proper registry.

* This includes all persons born in Spain, Cuba, Porto Rico, the Philippine Islands and other Spanish possessions.

† Members of the clergy are not eligible.

‡ This refers to physical or mental disability, and to disability through conviction of a crime, when the conviction carries with it the loss of political rights.

§ The incompatibility refers to holders of certain high office, resignation being required previous to seating in the Cortes.

ART. XVI. For the purposes of this law, when land is rented or land is cultivated on shares, two-thirds of the taxes shall be attributed to the landowner and one-third to the tenant or cultivator on shares. But the tenancy or the agreement to cultivate on shares must be proved by a certificate in writing recorded in the proper registry a year before the election. *[Certified Copies of Records.]*

The notaries public shall furnish without charge, upon free stamped paper,* copies of the documents to which this article and the foregoing one refer; and the officials of the register's office shall also, in the proper case, furnish free of charge and on like paper certified copies of the records and marginal notes. The object for which these documents are intended shall be stated therein, so that they may not be accepted by courts, district courts and Government offices for a purpose different from that intended by this decree.

ART. XVII. The following shall also have the right to be included in the registration lists, provided they have attained the age of twenty-five years: *[Persons Entitled to Registration.]*

1. Members of the Royal Spanish Academy and of the Royal Academies of History, of San Fernando, of Exact Sciences, of Physical and Natural Sciences, of Moral and Political Sciences, and of Medicine.

2. Members of ecclesiastical chapters, and parish priests and their curates.

3. Officials of all the departments of the Public Administration, of the Provincial Assemblies and of the municipalities, who shall have had a yearly salary of $100 for at least two years previous to registration; officials retired on pensions, whatever be the pension, and also retired heads of administrative departments, even if they be pensionless.

4. General officers of the army and admirals of the navy on furlough; chiefs† and military and navy officers retired on pension; soldiers, whether officers or privates, who have obtained the Cross of St. Fernando.‡

5. Persons who have obtained a professional diploma or academic degree, and shall have resided during the two years previous to registration within the limits of the municipality.

6. Painters and sculptors who have obtained a prize in a national or international exhibition.

7. Recorders and clerks of the court of the supreme courts and of the superior courts, notaries and attorneys, clerks of the court of district courts and members of commercial exchanges who come within the cases specified in Sections 1, 2, 3 and 4 of Art. VI.

ART. XVIII. The right to vote shall be denied to those whose cases shall fall within the contingencies specified in Sections 1, 2, 3 and 4 of Art. VI. *[Disqualifications for Voting.]*

---
* Before it was made also a source of revenue the object of the stamp was to prevent forgery. The stamp being numbered, a reference to the number was made in the body of the document, and the number of the stamp recorded separately. For some formalities, as in this case, the law directs the Government to furnish stamped paper free.

† In the Spanish army "jefe" (chief) is a generic term for colonel, lieutenant-colonel and major.

‡ This cross is awarded only to soldiers who have won distinction by heroic deeds in battle.

Those who are referred to in the second clause of Section 1, Art. V., of this decree shall exercise the right of suffrage only upon proof of compliance with the requirements for eligibility specified in that clause.

ART. XIX. The registration lists shall be completed in accordance with the foregoing provisions, and when so completed they shall constitute the standing electoral census.

VI.

PUBLIC MEETINGS AND ASSOCIATIONS.

Public Meetings only Restricted by Law.
Article XIII. of the Constitution gives the people the rights peaceably to assemble and to form associations. Of these rights no one may be deprived, unless the safety of the state require it, and the deprivation must be by virtue of some law, and only of a temporary nature. To enforce this article of the Constitution the Cortes passed two laws for the Peninsula: one, the act of June 15, 1880, to regulate the right of public meeting, and the other, the act of June 30, 1887, concerning the right of association. By royal decrees of November 1, 1881, and of June 12, 1888, these laws were extended to the island of Cuba.

The act regulating the right of peaceable assembly requires that the governor of the province in which a public meeting is to be held be given twenty-four hours' previous notice of the time and place of holding the meeting; it defines the meaning of "peaceable assembly"; it directs that a representative of the Government may be present at the meeting; and enumerates the cases in which the meeting may be suppressed.

Associations which Come within the Scope of the Law.
The act regulating the right of association refers to religious, political, scientific, social, artistic and eleemosynary associations, and to any other association not intended for purposes of profit. It refers also to guilds, mutual aid societies, associations of employers for the protection of employees, and to co-operative associations. This law does not refer to religious societies of the Catholic Church authorized by the Concordat* with the Pope. It does not refer to mercantile associations, these being regulated by other sections of the Civil Code or by the Commercial Code, nor to institutions and corporations created or governed by special legislation.

This act regulates the organization of associations, governs their relations with the state, and provides an office for their registration.

The decree extending this act to the island of Cuba made no noteworthy change in the law except in the clause referring to religious associations under the Concordat.

---

* An agreement between the Roman See and a secular government relative to matters that concern both.

VII.

THE GOVERNOR-GENERAL.

The Governor-General is the highest official of the island of Cuba. He is the supreme representative of the Government. His powers, except as now modified by the act of March 15, 1895, are contained in the following text: *Attributes of the Governor-General.*

Royal Decree of June 9, 1878.*

On motion of the Minister of the Colonies, and with the concurrence of the Council of Ministers, I decree as follows:

ARTICLE I. The Governor-General is the highest official representing the National Government in the island of Cuba. He is the delegate of the Ministers of the Colonies, of State, of War, and of the Navy. He has, moreover, as vice-royal patron, the powers inherent to the patronship of the Indies, agreeably with the papal bulls and the laws of the kingdom. His authority extends over all that conduces to the maintenance of the public peace, the preservation of the territory, the execution of the laws, and the protection of life and property.

He is the commander-in-chief of the army and navy of the island and controls the forces on land and sea, subject to the army and navy regulations. All the other authorities of the island are subordinate to him.

ART. II. His duties are: *His Duties.*

First. To publish and execute, in the provinces under his charge, the laws, decrees and orders, and the instructions of the Minister whose delegate he is, and the treaties and international conventions. To communicate, concerning foreign affairs, with her Majesty's consuls and diplomatic agents in America.

Second. To supervise and inspect all the branches of the state service in the island, and report to the Ministers he represents concerning their respective departments.

Third. To grant pardons whenever the urgency and gravity of the case and the impossibility of communication with the Peninsula* prevent him from consulting by letter or by telegraph upon the necessity and propriety of granting the pardon, in accordance with the orders of May 29, 1855, and the orders subsequent thereto.

Fourth. To apply, after previous deliberation with the Council of Authorities,† when extraordinary events, due to foreign or domestic causes which may menace or impair the security and defense of the land, occur, and when consultation with the Supreme Government would be dilatory, the law of April 17, 1821, or the Law of Public Peace, the latter law not being allowed to limit his powers under the former.

---
* Promulgated after the Zanjon Treaty.
† Spain proper is termed by Spaniards "the Peninsula," to distinguish it from Cuba, Porto Rico and the Philippine Islands, which are also "Spain."
‡ For Council of Authorities see Art. XII. of this law.

Fifth. When resolutions of the Madrid Government may occasion material or moral perturbations or seriously endanger the public welfare, owing to events that might occur upon such resolutions becoming known in the island, or owing to reasons the Government may not have taken into consideration, the Governor-General may suspend them. To decree such suspension the Council of Authorities must be heard, and notice of the suspension given to the Government as speedily as possible.

Sixth. To suspend for the same reasons the execution of the decisions of inferior officials, although such decisions might be within the powers of such officials, and would under ordinary circumstances be enforcible, explaining to the proper Minister the motives of the suspension, so that the matter may receive its due solution.

Other Obligations.

ART. III. It is incumbent also upon the Governor-General, as supreme chief of all the civil branches of the public administration:

First. To keep each branch of the public administration within the limits of its powers, as fixed by law.

Second. To publish edicts and take measures for the fulfillment of the laws and regulations and for the government of the island, giving notice thereof to the Minister of the Colonies.

Third. To propose to the Government measures to promote the moral and material welfare of the island, if such measures be not within the cognizance of the provincial or municipal authorities and corporations.

Fourth. To determine the penal institutions in which sentences shall be served, and to order the incarceration therein of convicts; and to designate also the jail liberties, when the courts may order confinement therein.

Fifth. To suspend delinquent public associations and municipal corporations.

Sixth. To order provincial governors to fine public functionaries and municipal corporations.

Seventh. To suspend, for cause justified by memorial, any public official whose appointment pertains to the Supreme Government, giving the Government immediate notice of such suspension, and to fill *pro tempore* the vacancy in accordance with the regulations now existing or hereafter to be provided.

Eighth. To grant or deny his permission to indict public officials, as provided by law.

ART. IV. The Governor-General shall exercise all the other functions of government that the laws may direct or that the Supreme Government may delegate to him.

ART. V. The Governor-General shall communicate directly with the Ministers whose delegate and representative he is. The departmental authorities shall communicate through him with their respective Ministers.

ART. VI. The Governor General may modify or revoke his decisions or those of his predecessors, unless they have been confirmed by the Government, or have vested rights, or have served as a basis for a judgment in a criminal or civil trial. Of his own motion he shall not modify or revoke his decision, when he bases the decision upon the limitation of his powers, or when the decision grants or denies permission for an indictment.

ART. VII. A decision of the Governor-General of a ministerial nature, or in a matter lying within his discretion, or when it assumes a reglamentary character, may be revoked or modified by the Supreme Government, whenever the latter may judge such decision contrary to the laws or general regulations, or injurious to the government and good administration of the island. His decision may also be revoked or modified on the appeal of a citizen deeming himself injured in his rights, provided the citizen be not required by law to obtain his remedy by proceedings before the council, before a municipal corporation, or before the Governor-General himself. *Means of Redress.*

ART. VIII. Objection to a decision of the Governor-General which determines the status of property must be before the mixed judicial and administrative court, as provided by law.

ART. IX. The Governor-General shall be appointed by royal decree issued by the President of the Council of Ministers, upon the proposition of the Minister of the Colonies. *How the Governor-General is Appointed.*

ART. X. He shall not surrender his charge nor absent himself from the island without the express order of the Government.

ART. XI. In case of the death of the Governor-General, his absence from the island, or inability to discharge the powers and duties of his office, the same shall devolve upon the Military Governor until the Government appoint a *pro tempore* substitute. *In Case of Death, Absence or Inability.*

If the absence be only from the capital of the island he shall continue discharging his duties from whatever place he may be in, and in matters of a ministerial nature, or matters within his exclusive competence, he may delegate his powers over each department to the respective heads thereof, but if the matter be within the competence of the Supreme Government its transaction must be through the Military Governor.

ART. XII. The Council of Superior Authorities, whose opinion in accordance with this decree the Governor-General must consult, is composed : of the Bishop of Havana, or the Archbishop of Santiago de Cuba, if the latter be present ; the Chief of the Naval Station ; the Military Governor ; the heads of the departments of Justice, of Finance, and of the Interior ; and the Attorney-General. *Council of Authorities.*

If, in the judgment of the Governor-General, the nature of the matters before the council requires the presence of the Provincial Governor the Governor-General may summon the Provincial Governor and give him a vote in the council.

The nature of this council is advisory. Its resolutions shall be drawn up in writing, signed by the members present, and certified to by the Secretary of the General Government, and inserted in a book provided for the purpose. A copy of each resolution shall be provided for each signatory, another for the Minister of the Colonies, and a copy for the Minister within whose department the matter treated of may fall. The Governor-General is free to follow or disregard the advice of the council. But following the advice of the council does not exempt him from the full responsibility for his acts. *The Council is Advisory.*

ART. XIII. All decrees inconsistent with the present decree are hereby revoked.

Done in the Palace, January 9, 1878.

            ALFONSO.

  The Minister of the Colonies,

         JOSÉ ELDUAYEN.

VIII.

PROVINCIAL ADMINISTRATION.

In 1878, the island having but recently been completely pacified, the Spanish Government deemed the time opportune to establish in Cuba the laws that under the Constitution of Spain gave all Spanish subjects equal rights. The mother country bore in mind that the growing extension and importance of the foreign trade of Cuba and its scientific and literary advances called for means of government different from those which had obtained. The state of revolt of the island, however, had made reform inadvisable.

The Island Divided Into Six Provinces.

By a royal decree of June 9 of the same year the island, for the purpose of administrative reorganization, was divided into six provinces, with a provincial governor for each province.

Another decree of June 21 of that year ordered the application, provisionally, in the island of Cuba of the organic provincial and municipal laws of 1870 of the Peninsula. These laws were made by a democratic Government* and slightly modified afterward. They determine all that which pertains to the civil administration of the Cuban provinces, to the organization, powers, and responsibilities of the provincial assemblies, and of the provincial officials, and to the estimates and accounts of the assemblies. Essentially the administration of the Cuban provinces is the same as that of the provinces of the Peninsula.

IX.

MUNICIPAL ADMINISTRATION.

The organization of municipalities in Cuba was regulated by the royal decree of July 27, 1859. Each municipality was provided with a board of aldermen for the administration of its affairs. Subsequently the decree was modified in some of its clauses by several other decrees, among these the royal decree of November 25, 1863, which organized the superior civil government of Havana, and the regulation of January 30, 1866, concerning the exercise of the powers appertaining to the civil governor of the province of Havana, in his double capacity of governor of the province and of president of the board of aldermen of the city, and with respect to the functions of the board.

Municipal Law Extended to Cuba.

Somewhat modified, the organic municipal law of the Peninsula of October 2, 1877, was extended to Cuba by the royal decree of

* In 1870 Spain was *de facto* a republic.

June 21, 1878. These modifications refer to the number of aldermen of each board and to the powers of the Governor-General in appointing mayors. Each mayor is appointed by the Governor-General from three nominees presented by the board of aldermen. The Governor-General may disregard the nominations of the boards and appoint as mayors persons not forming part of the municipalities. He also appoints assistant mayors, upon the nominations of the boards, the nominations being made in the same manner as in the case of the mayors. The nominees, however, must be members of the boards. .The salaries of mayors are municipal charges.

To recapitulate, the Governor-General exercises the functions which pertain by the law of the Peninsula to the Supreme Government, although with more amplitude. This amplitude is due to two reasons: First, to the slight experience of the Cuban people in public affairs; and, second, to the necessity, on account of the distance of the island from the Peninsula and the desire of avoiding expense and delay, of insuring freedom of action to the superior authority in the solution of local problems.

X.

PUBLIC PEACE.

The law of public peace of the Peninsula of April 23, 1873, is in force also in Cuba. It is applicable only after the suspension of constitutional rights as provided by the Constitution. With respect to the suspension of constitutional rights the present Constitution is the same as the democratic Constitution of 1869.* *Suspension of Constitutional Rights.*

This law gives the civil authorities extraordinary powers: To arrest citizens; to stop any publication; to disperse crowds, using force after the third request to disperse; to exile citizens; to compel a citizen to change his residence; and to enter private dwellings without warrant.

If these extraordinary powers prove insufficient the civil authorities may surrender their powers to the military authorities, and a state of siege may be proclaimed. *When Military Rule Can Be Proclaimed.*

Thereupon ordinary crimes are tried before the civil courts, but crimes of a seditious nature are tried before a court martial.

But under the protocol of January 7, 1877, between Spain and the United States, citizens of the United States must be tried before the civil courts, unless captured in arms.

* This Constitution was promulgated under the *de facto* republic which was established after the fall of Queen Isabel II. in 1868.

XI.
DEPARTMENT OF JUSTICE.

Jurisprudence. The metropolis has ever given its constant attention to this important department.

The early laws for the Indies contained wise and minute regulations for the administration of justice. For the same purpose numerous measures have been taken of late years. Among these are the royal decrees of January 30, 1855; of April 12, 1875; of May 23, 1879; of January 15, 1884, and of May 24, 1885.

At present the Revised Statutes of January 5, 1891, obtain. They contain, in methodical arrangement, the organic law of the Department of Justice for the colonial provinces and possessions. They refer to the division into judicial districts; to the appointment and promotion of magistrates, judges, state attorneys and clerks of the courts; to the judicial responsibility; to the jurisdictions of the various courts; to the inspection of the administration of justice; to the legal profession; and to all matters pertaining to the judicial organization and hierarchy.

The Departments of Justice of the Peninsula and of Cuba form an integral whole, the functionaries thereof being assimilated.

Administration of Justice in Cuba. There are in Cuba three territorial superior courts, of both civil and criminal jurisdiction, those of Havana, Santiago de Cuba, and Matanzas; three superior courts, of criminal jurisdiction only, those of Puerto Príncipe, Santa Clara and Pinar de Rio; and thirty-six inferior courts, of both criminal and civil jurisdiction, six in the city of Havana, two in the city of Matanzas, two in the city of Santiago de Cuba, and one in each of the following towns: Bejucal, Guanabacoa, Güines, Jaruco, Marianao, San Antonio de los Baños, Puerto Príncipe, Morón, Cañerias, Alfonso XII., Colón, Pinar del Rio, Guanajay, Guanes, San Cristóbal, Santa Clara, Cienfuegos, Sagua la Grande, San Juan de los Remedios, Sancti-Spiritu, Trinidad, Baracoa, Bayamo, Guantánamo, Holguin and Manzanillo.

XII.
CIVIL RIGHTS.

Cuba Enjoys the Same Rights as Spain. In this branch of the law the assimilation between Cuba and the Peninsula has been constant. The same substantive law and law of procedure obtains in both countries.

Shortly after its promulgation the Civil Code now in force in the Peninsula was, by the royal decree of July 31, 1889, integrally applied to the island of Cuba.

Thus Cubans were made participants in "an evident and extremely beneficent advance," for the Civil Code, as is felicitously stated in the preamble to the aforesaid royal decree, " reduces to one source the numerous dissimilar and conflicting fountains of the old Spanish civil law, modifies in a rational manner the law of inheritance, illumines and improves the law of personal rights and in general, with tradition as a basis, includes and regulates all classes of personal rights in a form that is more rational, more systematic and scientific than that effected by the laws which in so valuable and abundant a series have been bequeathed to us by former centuries."

And the Minister, D. Manuel Becerra, who subscribes this document, adds:

"Neither in the Spanish West Indies nor in the Philippine Islands is the civil law special or different from that which has been in force in the Peninsula, nor does the organization of the family and of property in those remote provinces demand any specialty in legislation for an existence whose evolution is exactly the same as that of the rest of the nation, because those peoples, although they have a genius proper to themselves and in some respects different from that of the people of Spain, adapted themselves long ago to the Spanish law, brought to them by the conquerors and missionaries.

" There exists therefore no danger of carrying to those countries rash innovations that might prove unwholesome to those communities, or changes that may be injurious to property, the title to which is acquired, maintained and alienated in the manner established by the old Spanish legislation, and that does not give rise to forms unknown among us and which it would be necessary to sanction by the law. And so the Colonial Committee on Codes made manifest to his Majesty's Government, when the Civil Code was discussed in the Chambers, the propriety of extending it to the colonial provinces as soon as it became law, without amendment either in the substance or in the form.

" And if it be indubitable that his Majesty may cherish the satisfaction of considering the enrichment of the nation with a civil code, that with so much anxiety and for so long a time it has solicited, as a happy event of his reign, no less indubitable is it that this sentiment of pure and elevating satisfaction will grow stronger and larger by extending the code to the colonial provinces, which with respect to this class of legislation have suffered the same inconveniences and will obtain the same advantages as the Peninsula.

" No constituent element of society knits a people together and binds them in the bosom of a common culture as the unity of legislation, and particularly of the civil law, which deals exclusively with the intimate relations of the lives and liberties of men.

"And if Spain was ever inspired in her policy toward the nations she ruled in another hemisphere by the lofty purposes of a paternalism, which was quickly to induce them to form a component part of this sublime and harmonious unity of the fatherland ; if Spain never applied to them a utilitarian and selfish system of government : if our history is filled with monuments that attest how the mother country never bartered away her desire generously to uplift and to draw to her bosom the inhabitants of the colonies, and to educate and rule them as she educated and ruled herself ; and if, as a happy result of this beneficent and self-sacrificing policy, the most important advantage that may be derived from legislation, which is identicalness in civil law, was established, it is both rational and politic to preserve that identicalness, maintaining thus our title to honor and securing the most priceless benefit that a nation can offer the peoples it rules, and which consists in establishing equality before the law and granting to all the subject nations the sum of the rights which she herself enjoys."

The Civil Procedure Act of September 25, 1885, of the Peninsula is also in force in Cuba. That law regulates the proceedings before both superior and inferior courts and the appeal to the Supreme Court at Madrid.

XIII.

THE LAW MERCHANT.

Various Laws for Promoting and Regulating Commerce.

By a royal decree of February 1, 1832, the Commercial Code of 1829 and the Code of Commercial Procedure of 1830 were extended to Cuba. The law of June 30, 1878, modified some clauses of the Commercial Code and suppressed others. This law was extended to Cuba by the royal decree of November 1, 1878.

The act of November, 1869, now in force in the Peninsula, concerning the bankruptcy of railway and public works companies, was extended to Cuba on August 12, 1881.

The Commercial Code of August 22, 1885, of the Peninsula was also extended to Cuba by a royal decree of January 28, 1886. Thus was the greatest freedom for commercial transactions granted to the island of Cuba.

On August 16, 1878, a regulation for the organization of stock companies in the colonial provinces was approved. A royal decree of the same date ordered that banks of issue and discount be governed by that regulation. Under that decree a bank was established for the island of Cuba and was given the monopoly of the issue of bank notes. This bank is similar to the Bank of

Spain, in the Peninsula, and is governed by an administrator, a governor and two vice-governors, all appointed by the Supreme Government.

XIV.
MORTGAGES.

By a royal decree of May 16, 1879, the Law of Mortgages that obtains in the Peninsula was extended to Cuba. This act went into operation on May 1, 1880. Some changes had been made in the law, but they gave undesirable results. Reforms Adopted.

To avoid these undesirable results, and to harmonize this act with the Civil Code, which had been subsequently introduced in 1889, and with other existing laws, the act was modified by the law of July 14, 1893.

This last act provides facilities for the registration of land titles, guaranteeing their ownership, and cheapening the registration of small holdings; it gives the seller of agricultural machinery and implements a lien for the full purchase price upon the articles sold, and, with the consent of the buyer, a lien upon the latter's land; it also simplifies the foreclosure of mortgages, and so forth.

There are in Cuba twenty-five land registry offices, situated in the following towns: Havana, Cárdenas, Matanzas, Pinar del Rio, Bejucal, Cienfuegos, Guanajay, Puerto Principe, Santa Clara, Santiago de Cuba, Trinidad, Sagua la Grande, Alfonso XII., Baracoa, Bayamo, Colón, Guanabacoa, Güines, Holguin, Jaruco, Manzanillo, San Antonio de los Baños, San Cristóbal, San Juan de los Remedios and Sancti-Spiritu.

XV.
REGISTRY AND CIVIL MARRIAGE.

The royal decree of January 8, 1884, and the regulation of November 8 of the same year extended to Cuba and to Porto Rico the act of June 17, 1870, with some modifications due to the peculiarities of those islands. This act regulates civil registry in the Peninsula, and ordains all that which pertains to the civil status[*] of citizens. Civil Registry Regulated.

The parish records were transcribed to the register,[†] and provisional inscriptions were made in cases in which citizens were unable to exhibit certificates of birth.

---
[*] Civil status (*estado civil*) is the *état civil* of the French. It means the civil condition of a citizen with respect to being of age or under age, married or unmarried, legitimate or illegitimate.

[†] This register corresponds to the American bureaus of vital statistics, which keep a record of births, deaths and marriages.

This act became a valuable protection to the freedom of emancipated slaves, and is a proof of the honesty with which the laws for the abolition of slavery in Cuba were enforced.

Civil Marriage Act Extended to Cuba. The Civil Marriage Act of the Peninsula of June 18, 1870, and the royal decree of February 9, 1875, modifying this act, are a development of Art. XI. of the Constitution, which guarantees freedom of worship.*

The Constitution having been proclaimed in Cuba and Porto Rico on April 7, 1881, the Marriage Act and decree aforesaid were necessarily extended to Cuba and Porto Rico. This gave all residents of these islands, Spanish subjects and foreigners alike, the right, irrespective of their religious faith, to contract matrimony.

Spain has ever furthered the social needs of the dwellers within her boundaries. Thus the royal order of December 16, 1792, provided a form of civil marriage and registry for the marital unions contracted in the territories of Florida and Louisiana, at that time Spanish possessions, between Protestants, or between Catholics and Protestants.

The provisions of Chapter III. of the Civil Code of October 6, 1888, concerning civil marriage, which obtain in the Peninsula, were extended to Cuba and Porto Rico by the royal decree of July 31, 1889, and now obtain in those islands.

XVI.

NOTARIES.†

From the time of the laws for the Indies notaryships in Cuba were gifts within the grant of the Crown, the duties thereof being discharged by the grantee or his deputy.

Notaryships Regulated. By the act of March 3, 1873, the Government was ordered to regulate notaryships in the colonies in accordance with the law of May 28, 1862, which obtained in the Peninsula, and which was one of the best in Europe. The present law of notaryships for Cuba and Porto Rico was proclaimed on October 29, 1874. It is adapted to the special needs of those islands, and is based upon the experience obtained by the working of the law in the Peninsula. It has exalted the office of notary into a profession, and divided the territory into notarial districts, thereby facilitating the making of contracts.

---

* Formerly only canonical marriages (*i. e.*, marriages solemnized under the rites of the Church of Rome) were recognized. The Constitution having established religious toleration this law recognizes the validity of non-Catholic marriages.

† In Spanish countries, as in France, the notary is an important official, whose functions include conveyancing, &c.

XVII.

CRIMINAL LAW.

Until the year 1878 the old penal laws of Spain were applied in Cuba, the courts being allowed in certain cases to mitigate the harshness of the law.

A Spanish democratic legislature passed a Penal Code on June 17, 1870. That code, as subsequently amended at the suggestions of a revising commission of jurists, now obtains in the Peninsula. With its amendments it was extended to the island of Cuba by a royal decree of May 23, 1879. *Revised Penal Code of Spain Extended to Cuba.*

In establishing in Cuba the Penal Code of the mother country no alteration was introduced in the text except such changes as were required by the exigencies of the conditions peculiar to the colonial provinces, and the innovations demanded by the Constitution, the proclamation of the Constitution having been subsequent to that of the Code of the Peninsula. The chief modifications are due to the necessity of providing the Governor-General with powers analogous to those of the Supreme Government of the Peninsula ; to the absolute inapplicability of the law, as in the case of offenses committed in the Royal Palace, or in the Houses of Parliament at Madrid ; to the difference in climate ; and to the necessity of securing the right of masters over their slaves* and freedmen.† Cuba has now a criminal code upon a scientific basis and in accordance, in the matter of crimes and penalties, with the teachings of modern schools of criminalogists.

Rules of criminal procedure were established for the application of this code, and an appeal to the Supreme Court at Madrid provided. Thus the criminal law of the colonies was assimilated to that of the Peninsula, and the natives of Cuba were conceded the protection of appeal to the highest tribunal of the kingdom. *Criminal Procedure and Right of Appeal.*

Moreover, by the royal decree of October 19, 1878, the Criminal Procedure Act of September 14, 1882, which obtains in the Peninsula, with some amendments suggested by the Colonial Committee on Codes, was extended to Cuba. This act establishes trial by indictment and in open court.

The foregoing shows that the penal laws, both substantive law and law of procedure, now in force in Cuba protect the life of the citizen and the security of society, and are agreeable to the modern views of this important branch of legislation.

---
* Slavery was totally abolished in 1886.
† Freedmen (*libertos*) were emancipated slaves. Certain mutual rights and duties of no practical importance, such as the duty of mutual assistance in case of poverty, &c., remained.

XVIII.

PUBLIC INSTRUCTION.

Public Instruction Fostered.
This important department, the foundation of a people's culture and prosperity, has in Cuba always received the most careful attention. As far back as 1680 we find in Title 22, Book 1 of the Codified Laws of the Indies judicious precepts which show how great was the interest taken by Spanish monarchs in public instruction in the colonies.

In recent years, as formerly, the idea of unification with the legislation of Spain has prevailed in the legislation relating to this department. The decree of July 5, 1863, extended to Cuba the act of September 9, 1857, which is still in force in the Peninsula, and the greater part of the regulations prescribed for its enforcement.

Havana University Faculties.
Still with the intent of unification, by the decree of June 18, 1880, important reforms were effected. By the decree of December 7 of the same year the plan of instruction was reorganized. Faculties of sciences, of philosophy and the humanities, of medicine, of pharmacy and of law, were formed in the University of Havana, thus creating in the latter the same faculties which compose the University of Madrid. An Institute* like the institutes of the Peninsula, and with the same curriculum and government, was established in each of the six provinces of Cuba.

By the royal decree of July 7, 1883, the Havana University District was created in the same form as the districts established in the Peninsula, the rector of the University of Havana being the head of all the educational establishments of the district. The decree of July 5, 1887, regulated the process, which is the same as that of the Peninsula, to enable the university to confer decrees for studies conducted privately.

The Governor-General of Cuba appoints all the primary† school instructors whose salaries exceed $300 a year; the others are appointed by the rector of the University of Havana.

Representation in the Superior Board of Public Instruction.
For the supervision of public education there is in Madrid the Superior Board of Public Instruction, whose members are partly appointees of the crown and partly elective. Among the former is the Under Secretary of the Colonial Department and among the latter

---
* Institutes (*institutos*) are Government schools of second education (see note below), in contradistinction from the private schools of second education (*colegios*).

† In Spanish countries schools are divided into schools of first (*i. e.*, primary) education and schools of second (*i. e.*, higher) education.

The course of the schools of higher education is of five years, an A. B. being obtained at the completion of this course. This degree is, however, only a preparation to matriculation in the universities and in the professional schools.

five members selected by the colonial provinces. Of these five members Cuba chooses two and has due representation in that high consultive body of the kingdom, the similarity, or rather the equality, which has on this point existed for a long time past between Cuba and the Peninsula being patent.

XIX.
ECONOMICS.

Besides granting to Cuba, with other political rights, the right to representation in the national parliament—a privilege which England has conceded to none of her colonies—Spain has kept making concessions advantageous to the interests of her West Indian provinces, even when such concession seemed contrary to the interests of the Peninsula. Scarcely had peace been made with France and Ferdinand VII. been restored to his throne when two royal decrees were proclaimed; one for the encouragement of white immigration and the other to open the ports of Cuba to the flags of all nations. In a few years the economic situation of the island completely changed. Prior to the promulgation of the decrees the Cuban treasury had required the constant aid of the treasury of the colony of Mexico. From 1850 to 1860 the Cuban treasury was in so prosperous a state that with only a tax of 2 per cent. on the produce of rural property and of 4 per cent. on the rentals of urban real estate, a small tax on the sale of realty, the stamp tax, and the customs dues, which had greatly increased owing to the thriving condition of trade, its surplus never fell below $3,000,000, while it rose for some years to $5,000,000, although for some time the treasury made a yearly contribution of $2,000,000 to the Crown.

Period of Prosperity.

The favorable state of affairs ceased after 1860. The failure of many stock companies which had abused their credit, and the facilities afforded by the Government, with the intention of developing the natural resources of the country, to mercantile and industrial associations, caused an intense depression, the effect of which was felt by the public treasury. Filibustering attempts against the sovereignty of Spain previous to 1868, and the rebellion of 1868–1878, which broke out at the very moment of the proclamation in Spain of a democratic constitution that was a guarantee of a liberal government for the Spanish West Indies,* caused a large increase in the estimates for the army and the navy, which previously had been very slight, and further embarrassed the treasury.

Increase in Appropriations Due to the Rebellion.

If some years later the prosperity of the island was again affected it was partly owing to an increase in the cost of production, due to

---
* Universal suffrage was established in Porto Rico at the same time that it was established in Spain, in 1870.

the abolition of slavery and to the exclusion of Cuban sugar from several foreign markets, and partly owing to an increase in the production of beet sugar, circumstances over which the Government had no control.

Convention Called to Discuss Financial and Other Matters.

Previous to 1868 public opinion on the island had been much occupied with the economic problems. The Government had already sought to increase the supply of field laborers, which was growing scarce owing to the suppression of the slave trade, by permitting the importation of Chinese coolies. Finally it convoked in Madrid delegates from the Spanish West Indies for the discussion of colonial questions from all points of view, including the political.

The delegates met in assembly, expounded their views and presented plans, which, to be sure, differed much among themselves, upon the questions submitted to them, such as the facilitation of immigration, the treaties of commerce it was desirable to make, and a system of taxation more in harmony with the needs of the island.

It was to the initiative of the actual president of the Council of Ministers, D. Antonio Canovas del Castillo, that the convocation of the delegates was due.

Taxation Considerably Reduced.

When the revolt of 1868 broke out the first preparatory measures were taken for the suppression of slavery and for the consequent change to a new labor system, the change being accomplished without the perturbations that have afflicted the colonies of other nations. New tariffs, to the advantage both of the consumer of imports and of the native producer, were tried, and if then, as afterward, the exigencies of the war increased all taxation, on the conclusion of peace the Government, with the assent of the Cuban representative in the Cortes, hastened to lower the taxes to the normal rate, the tax on the products of rural property falling to a rate lower than that in any country of European origin.*

At the request of the representatives of Cuba, who were desirous of extending the Cuban market in the Peninsula, a Navigation and Customs Act was passed in 1882. The object of the statute was to unify gradually the commerce of Spain and Cuba, so that vessels trading between the Peninsula and the island might have all the privileges of a coastwise trade. A few duties, however, were to be restored, for no nation is under obligation to sacrifice its exchequer in order to increase the growth of the wealth of its colonies. That has never been done by France, nor by England, who, in that respect, deals with her colonies as with foreign nations. Still less by Holland, who exploits her colonial possessions.

Relief Measures for Sugar Producers.

Since 1884, when the great depression in the sugar trade of Cuba and Porto Rico began, owing to the exclusion of their sugars from all markets save that of the United States, and to combinations of

---

* See Appendix.

American refiners to reduce the price of that staple, no rational measure for the relief of Cuban sugar producers has been proposed by the Cuban deputies which has not been gladly accepted by the Cortes and by the Government, the Prime Minister, Sr. Canovas del Castillo, declaring it was necessary for the Peninsula to make great sacrifices to the needs of the colonial provinces.

Vessels sailing under the United States flag were conceded the same privileges as those sailing under the Spanish flag in exchange for the non-application by the United States of extraordinary duties on Cuban sugars, the concession proving a serious injury to the producers of the Peninsula and to her shipping interests, both through the decrease in home freights and later through the loss of other carrying trade. *Concessions Made to the United States Prove Injurious to Home Interests.*

The estimates of expenditures of the Government in Cuba were steadily lowered.* They were stripped of all items that were not of absolute necessity, although plausible reasons were not lacking for the retention of some of the items suppressed. The army and the navy were reduced to a size smaller than was required for the defense of the island, and for the anticipation of events that were not slow to occur.

The export tax on sugar—a valuable source of revenue—was abolished, with the intention of benefiting the producer.*

The import tax on Cuban and Porto Rican sugar was abolished in the Peninsula, leaving only the town dues, the duty on foreign sugar being considerably raised.

A treaty of commerce and navigation was negotiated with the United States for the exclusive benefit of the producers and of the trade of Cuba and Porto Rico. In this treaty the interests of producers of the Peninsula were made a secondary consideration, and the manufacturers of flour, and consequently the wheat raisers, of the mother country were sacrificed. Owing to a change of administration in the United States the treaty was not ratified. Five years later, however, it was again negotiated and was ratified, remaining in operation as long as the United States consented. *Effects of the Reciprocity Treaty with the United States.*

So great was the injury to producers and to the trade of the Peninsula that one article, flour, the exportation of which to Cuba and Porto Rico constituted for many years the wealth of a vast district, was excluded from the Spanish West Indian market.

The interest on the Cuban debt was considerably reduced. Previously the debt had been guaranteed by the Cuban custom dues; now the Cuban debt is guaranteed by Spain. Thus it became possible to recall the bank notes issued during the war of 1868-1878. *Cuban Debt Guaranteed by Spain.*

Finally, when by the termination of the commercial treaty with the United States American products were placed at a disadvantage

*See Appendix.

in their competition with the products of the Peninsula, because the Navigation Act gave the products of the latter the advantage, some measures favorable to the products of the United States were taken and others prepared though not voted on account of the adjournment of the Cortes.

Tariff Reform under Consideration.
At the present moment reforms in the tariff law of the Spanish West Indies are under consideration.* The intent is to conciliate as far as possible the interests of the native producer and consumer with the requirements of a revenue derived mainly from customs dues, by the desire, directly or indirectly expressed, of the inhabitants of Cuba and Porto Rico, to whom taxes on real estate and on manufactures are repugnant.

Cuban Taxation Lower than in Other Countries.
The taxes which constitute the estimated revenue of the island of Cuba for 1895–6 are not heavier, and in some cases are lighter, than taxes in other countries.

The sources of revenues, exclusive of customs, are the taxes on the sale of realty ; on mining claims ; on urban real estate (12 per cent. on the rental†) ; on rural real estate (2 per cent. on the value of the produce‡); on manufactures ; on licenses to sell goods ; on licenses to practice the learned professions ; on licenses to practice trades ; on consumption of liquors and on licenses to sell liquors ; on the sale of railway tickets (1 per cent.); on tobacco ; on the consumption of petroleum ; on the salaries of employees of the state, and on certain payments by the state (1 per cent.) ; and a capitation tax.

Tariff and Surcharge.
The import duties consist of the imposts fixed by a schedule and a surcharge.§

The law of June 30, 1892, made the surcharge 10 per cent. on all articles except articles of food and a few other articles. The law of June 28, 1895, increased the surcharge to 15 per cent. and extended the list of exempt articles.

Various other indirect taxes, amounting to 20 per cent. of the estimated revenue, complete the list of taxes.

Good Effects of Peace.
From the time of the pacification of the island in 1878 to the outbreak of the present insurrection production, trade, navigation, railways and population considerably increased.§

* A committee of the Chambers of Commerce of Havana, Santiago de Cuba and Cienfuegos was summoned to Madrid to present the views of the merchants of the island on tariff matters.

† On the *net* rental after deduction of all expenses.

‡ This is also on the *net* produce. Thus for some years 60 per cent. of the market price of coffee was allowed for expenses of production.

§ See Appendix.

XX.
CUBA'S PUBLIC DEBT.

Until 1868 the finances of the island of Cuba were in an exceedingly prosperous condition. For many years there was an excess of revenue over expenditure, although, as has been said before, the Cuban treasury made large contributions to the national treasury. In spite of the fact that the cost of the military expeditions to Mexico and San Domingo was defrayed by the Treasury, the deficit at the outbreak of the Cuban revolt in 1868 was only $7,630,000, an insignificant sum in view of the resources of the island. That these burdens were thrown upon the Cuban treasury is not surprising, inasmuch as for many years the Crown of Spain had in Cuba a very costly colony, whose expenses had to be met by subsidies from the colonies of Mexico and Peru. *Financial Straits Caused by the Insurrection.*

It was but reasonable to suppose that in the following year, if the whole deficit could not be paid, at least the great excess of revenue over expenditures of the previous years would not fail, but from the outbreak of the revolt such hopes were vain.

The revenues, in consequence of the revolt, were much reduced, while the expenses rose to huge proportions. Extraordinary taxes were levied, but they proved insufficient. Loans were obtained first from the Banco Español of Havana and subsequently from other banks. Treasury notes and bank notes guaranteed by the Treasury, the latter through the Banco Español of Havana, were issued. The Treasury issued bonds guaranteed by the customs dues, and a floating debt for the liquidation of previous expenditures was formed. All these debts were consolidated by the issues of bonds guaranteed by the Cuban treasury to the amount of 620,000,000 pesetas ($124,000,000) in 1886, and to the amount of 222,500,000 pesetas ($44,500,000) in 1890, making a total debt at the outbreak of the present revolt of $168,500,000. *Consolidation of the Debt.*

The sources of the Cuban debt being shown, all commentary is unnecessary.

Porto Rico has never risen in revolt. It has no debt.

XXI.
APPOINTMENTS TO PUBLIC OFFICE.
RIGHTS OF CUBANS.

No law deprives Cubans of the right, in common with other Spanish citizens, to hold public office. *Cubans Hold Public Offices.*

They hold office, on equal terms with the natives of the Peninsula, in the civil administration, the judiciary, the army, the navy and the church.* If there be any inequality it is to their advantage.

This may be easily proved by the preamble of the royal decree of October 13, 1890, for the reorganization of the administrative personnel appointed by the Minister of the Colonies, and by other resolutions. The decree very properly recites that "from the time of the old laws of the Indies Spanish legislation has tended to obliterate the differences of origin between the natives of the colonial provinces and of the Peninsula, equalizing their rights and granting the former direct participation in state offices.

"The development of this policy," it adds, "has produced the result that public offices are filled indiscriminately by Spaniards of the Peninsula and by Spaniards of the colonial provinces. With that end in view, the present laws afford means, sure in some grades of the administration and easy in others, that place within the reach of all officials the offices which form the graduated scale of the administrative bodies."

Fifth Officers Mostly Cubans. That decree gives the Governor-General the power to appoint all officials whose salaries are above 1,500 pesetas ($300), that is to say inclusive of fifth officers.† The great majority of these fifth officers are natives of the colonial provinces, owing to the requirement, among others, for appointment of a residence in the territory during at least the *two years* previous to entrance upon the discharge of the duties. Thus all fifth officers in Cuba must have resided on the island during at least the two years previous to entering office.

The following is the text:

Qualifications Required. ART. XVII. The appointments of fifth officers in the colonial provinces shall be made by the respective Governor-Generals, giving immediate notice to the Minister of the Colonies for confirmation, by royal order, of the appointments.

The appointment shall state the appointee's qualifications, and verify them by documentary proof thereof.

Said qualifications are:

1. Residence in the respective territories for the two years previous to appointment.

2. To be eighteen years of age.

3. To have filled an office of the same grade,‡ without reprimand, in the central or provincial administration; or to have held a clerk-

---

* The Archdeacon of the Cathedral of Porto Rico, D. Baldomero Hernandez, is a native of the Spanish West Indies. So are several priests who occupy high offices, among them the Prebendary of the Cathedral of Havana, D. Mariano Rodriguez Armenteros.

† Employment in the public administration is in Spain, as in France, a profession organized in ranks. The lowest rank, which corresponds to second lieutenant in the army, is the fifth officer; the fourth officer, third officer, &c., being above him. An official, if discharged, is still in the profession, and is in a situation analogous to that of an army officer placed on furlough.

‡ *I. e.*, if a fifth officer, he must have held a fifth officer's position.

ship, with the same qualification as to reprimand, and to have had for four years a yearly salary of $300 in Porto Rico and in the Philippine Islands, and of $600 in Cuba ; or to have obtained the degree of bachelor of arts or a professional diploma of some kind.

With regard to offices of greater importance the natives of the colonial provinces are truly privileged. Another article of the same decree says :

ART. XIII. *Residents of the islands of Cuba, Porto Rico and the Philippines* who have been provincial deputies, or have been mayors or aldermen of a provincial capital, or have been members of administrative councils or members of the present consultive or auxiliary administrative boards in the capitals of provinces, may be appointed as heads of administrative departments, excepting the customs, in their respective provinces ; and those who have been members of provincial and local boards, or been mayors or aldermen of municipalities, excepting the provincial capitals, may be appointed as heads of departmental sections, provided they have the following qualifications : Cubans as Heads of Departments.

1. *Residence in their respective territories during the eight years preceding* the appointment.
2. To have held for four years, without having resigned, one of the offices enumerated in this article.

If the office be that of provincial assemblyman, mayor or alderman, it must have been obtained through a popular election.*

The proportion of offices in each branch of the national administration held by natives of the colonial provinces is the best evidence of the liberality with which their merits and abilities have been rewarded.

The present Minister of War, Lieutenant-General D. Marcelo de Azcarraga y Palmero, is a native of the Philippine Islands.

The ex-Minister of the Colonies, D. Buenaventura de Abarzuza, is a Cuban. The Under Secretary of the Colonial Department, D. Guillermo de Osma, is also a Cuban. So are D. Wenceslao Ramirez de Villaurrutia, the late Assistant Secretary of State, and D. Francisco Cassa, the present Secretary of the Province of Madrid. Cubans in High Office in Spain.

D. Francisco Lastres, Vice-President of the Chamber of Deputies in the last legislature, and D. Santos Guzman, another ex-Vice-President of the Chambers, are Cubans.

In the diplomatic service there are a number of Cubans. D. Lorenzo de Castellanos was the Minister that represented Spain in Mexico.

The long list of employees of the colonial civil service contains, together with the names of Cubans who took part in the former revolt, and who held office either in the metropolis or on the island, the names of many natives of Cuba, among them : Acosta, Montalvo, Azcárate, Vinent, Kindelan, Freire, Ilisástegui, Echevarria, Justiz, Saladrigas, O'Farril, Bolivar, Rosillo, Valdés, Malli, Armas, Betan-

---

* This would exclude appointees to fill vacancies.

court, Bernal, Balboa, Cadaval, Diago, Chacón, Beltrán, Insua, Kohaly, Varona, and scores of others.

In the Post Office Department alone there are more than 100 Cubans, that is to say, one-half of the total number of officials.

Department of Education in the Hands of Cubans.
The Department of Education may be said to be in the hands of Cubans. The Rector of the University of Havana, D. Joaquin F. Lastres, is a Cuban. Cubans also are the Vice-Rector, D. José Maria Carbonell, the Secretary-General, D. Juan Gomez de la Maza y Tejada, and the deans of all the faculties: D. José Castellanos y Arango, dean of the faculty of philosophy and the humanities; D. Manuel J. Cañizales Benegas, dean of the faculty of sciences; D. Leopoldo Berrier y Fernandez, dean of the faculty of law; D. Federico Hortsman y Cantos, dean of the faculty of medicine; D. Carlos Donoso y Lardier, dean of the faculty of pharmacy; and the director of the botanic gardens, D. Manuel Gomez. Of the eighty professors of the university sixty are Cubans.

The director, D. Bruno Garcia Ayllon, and the eight other professors of the School of Technology are Cubans. Of the three instructors of the School of Painting and Sculpture only one is a native of the Peninsula, the director being a Cuban. The institutes of Matanzas, Santa Clara and Puerto Principe are under the direction of Cubans, D. Eduardo Diaz y Martinez, D. Alejandro Muxo y Pablos and D. Agustin Betancourt y Ronquillo respectively.

The total number of professors of all the institutes of the island is fifty-eight. Of that number thirty-five are Cubans.

The Department of Justice Mostly Intrusted to Cuban Magistrates.
In the Department of Justice of the island nearly all the offices of lower rank* are held by natives. With extremely rare exceptions the municipal judges and district attorneys are Cubans. Even in the higher ranks of the magistracy the natives have a large share of the offices. The justices of the Supreme Court of Havana, D. Manuel Vias Ochoteco, D. Francisco Noval y Marti and D. Juan Valdés Pagés, are natives of the Spanish West Indies. So are D. José Maria Larrazabal, presiding justice of the Supreme Court of Matanzas; D. Francisco Ramos y Moya, presiding justice of the Supreme Court of Santiago de Cuba, and D. Belisario Alvarez Céspedes, assistant district attorney of Havana.

Of forty-one justices of the Supreme Courts ten are Cubans; of twenty-four judges of the Courts of Criminal Appeal seven are Cubans; of thirty-six district court judges† (*de término*) twelve are

---
* See note below.

† The judiciary in Spain, as in France, is a profession organized in ranks, the lowest rank being the district court judge of entry (*juez de entrada*), and the highest the presidency of the Supreme Court (*presidente de la audiencia*). The profession is open only to members of the bar, entrance being by competitive examination and promotion by seniority. Above the district court judge (*de entrada*) ranks the judge (*de ascenso*), and above the latter the judges (*de término*).

44

Cubans; of forty-four district court judges (*de ascenso*) thirteen are Cubans; of sixty-two district court judges (*de entrada*) twenty-three are Cubans, and in the Philippine Islands seven Cubans hold judicial offices. There are therefore in the judicial profession in the colonial provinces seventy-eight natives of those provinces; that is to say, *thirty per cent.* of the total. And this ratio will increase in favor of the natives of the colonial provinces, for the facilities for the admission of natives to the judiciary have much increased in recent years, and many who are now in the lower ranks of the judiciary will in time rise through promotion by seniority.

Of the seventy-five notary districts fifty are in charge of Cubans. Of twenty-five land registry offices thirteen are in charge of Cubans.

Cuba has a large and brilliant representation in the Spanish army. Major-General D. José Arderius, who but a few months ago was military governor of Havana, is a Cuban. So are Major-Generals D. Andres Gonzales Muñoz and D. Francisco Loño, who are serving now in Cuba, and Major General D. Adolfo Rodriguez Bruzon, who is stationed in the Peninsula. Brigadier-Generals D. Emiliano Loño, D. Miguel Bosch, D. Jorge Garrich, D. Juan Godoy, and others are also natives of the Spanish West Indies.

Distinguished Cuban Officers in the Spanish Army.

The Spanish army has had many famous commanders of colonial origin. Captain-Generals D. José Manuel Gutierrez de la Concha and D. Manuel Gutierrez de la Concha were natives of Buenos Ayres; Captain-General D. Juan Zavala was a native of Peru; Captain-General Juan de la Pezuela, who still lives, is a native of Peru; Lieutenant-General D. Felipe Rivero was a native of Bolivia; D. Antonio Ros de Olano was a native of Caracas; D. Fernando Fernandez de Córdova was a native of Buenos Ayres; Lieutenant-Generals D. Ramon Zarco del Valle, D. Vicente Genaro de Quesada and D. Joaquin de Ezpeleta were natives of Havana; Major-Generals D. Juan Ampudia, D. Felix Ferrer and D. Francisco Acosta were natives of Cuba.

In the infantry, chiefs* and officers who are natives of the colonial provinces are numerous. Among them are Garcia Delgado, Aguilera, Padilla, Romaguera, Sanchez Echevarria, Gaston, Rubio Masot, Salas Marzal, Lopez Rozabal, Marti, Castilla Mármol, Alvarado, Villalón, Amoedo, Infante, Cevallos Avilés, Luque, Loperena, Garriga, Mahy, &c.

Infantry Officers.

In the cavalry, although the personnel is smaller, the number of chiefs and officers who are natives of the Spanish West Indies is nearly one hundred. Among them are Girond, Zapirain, Figueroa, Yrio, Urgelles, Andriani, Palanca, Serrano Dominguez, Pezuela, Vinent, Moreno, Fromista, Gonzalez Anleo, Roviralta, Gamboa,

Cavalry Officers.

* See note page 23.

Gregorich, Betancourt, Perez Pedroso, Obregón Fedriani, Kirpatrich, O'Farril and others.*

Cuban Officers in Other Corps.

In the artillery the number of chiefs and officers natives of the colonial provinces is fifty-five. Among them are Flores, Segarra, Tapia Ruano, Ceballos, Planell, Velay Silva, Garcia del Valle, Vicario y Delfin, Osma y Scull, Marchesi, De Miguel, Valdivia, Irizar, Vega y Zayas and others.

In the engineers the number of officers natives of the colonial provinces is thirty-six. Among them are Otero Cossio, Gayoso y O'Nagthen, Portillo, Navarro y Muzquiz, Kindelan, Manzano, Dominicis, Casamitjana, Tuero, Gonzalez Estefani and others.

In the general staff there are nineteen natives of the colonial provinces. Among them are Castañera, Domingo, Kindelan, Vivanco, Casariego, Incenga, Morales, Ortiz and others.

In the constabulary the number of natives of the colonial provinces is thirty-five ; in the custom house the number is nine ; in the military sanitary corps thirteen ; in the military administration seventeen ; in the judge advocate's office two ; in the veterinary corps, two.

The navy list also includes colonial born admirals and officers.

Cubans Take Part in National Legislation.

The natives of Cuba and Porto Rico have free access to all the official careers. They have their share, without restriction, in the national life in all its aspects. Cubans and Porto Ricans, as representatives of their provinces in the Senate and in the Chamber of Deputies, take part in the legislation for the whole Spanish nation.†

---

* In the infantry and cavalry alone now serving in the war in Cuba there are 146 officers of all ranks, from major-general to second lieutenant, who are natives of Cuba. If to that number be added the officers serving in the artillery and the engineers and in the ordnance, medical and commissary departments, it would be a sober statement to say that 500 Cuban officers are now in the Spanish army fighting against the rebellion. All these officers have passed through the Spanish military academies, and not a single one of them has deserted the Spanish flag.

† A famous man of letters, D. Juan Valera, ex-Minister of Spain to the United States, has very properly said in an article recently published in Madrid :

"I maintain that we have at all times, from the remote past, given Spanish Americans every proof of our esteem and affection. * * * The fact that they were Spanish Americans did not in the slightest degree militate against Gorostiza, Ventura de la Vega, Rafael Maria Baralt, and José Heriberto Garcia de Quevedo ; on the contrary, they received the highest encomiums in Spain ; we applauded them and honored them with important posts and offices. Many other illustrious men, likewise born in Spanish America, have become Spanish statesmen and generals. Among these may be cited the Marquis del Duero. All those who have distinguished themselves in Spanish America by their learning, their genius and their exploits, since the time when Spanish America became independent, have been as famous and have been praised and admired as much in Spain as in the republics which gave them birth. Take as instances Don Andrés Bello, whom we all admire as a philologist and as the author of 'International Law,' and whose beautiful and polished verses we know from memory ; Don Rufino Cuervo, whose dictionary we regard as a marvel of industry. And how greatly do we admire the poems of the two Caros, and those of Marmol, Andrade, Obligado, Restrepo, Oyuela, Ruben Dario and many others !"

XXII.

GOVERNMENT PROFESSIONS.*

On September 20, 1878, at the suggestion of the President of the Council of Ministers, at that time D. Antonio Canovas del Castillo, a royal decree was proclaimed ordering that the personnels of the courts of justice, universities, institutes, special schools, normal schools, and primary schools should each constitute one profession whose members would serve without discrimination in the Peninsula and in the colonial provinces.

Unification of Civil Professions.

That was at the time of the Zanjon capitulation. As was then said by the president of the council: "Since the pacification of Cuba, your Majesty's Government has not ceased its efforts to afford the colonial provinces the benefits of a normal situation, by establishing in each of them the provincial and municipal organization best fitted to its needs, and by encouraging immigration and insuring the stability of the credit of the island, an indispensable element to the growth of a nation's wealth.

"In the task of reconstruction and assimilation there is lacking an important reform, a reform which will contribute effectually to tighten the bonds between the various parts of the Spanish territory and will further the establishment of recent legislation. This reform is the unification of the civil professions in the Peninsula and in the colonial provinces. Formerly they were unified, but a narrow interpretation of the law has separated them, to the injury both of the officials and of the administration of the government. All the services are not disconnected in so singular a manner. The army, the navy, the civil engineers of roads and canals, of mines and forests, and the telegraphists serve, without discrimination, in Spain, in the Spanish West Indies, in the Philippine Islands and in the possessions of the Gulf of Guinea. Only the personnels of the courts of justice, of public instruction, and of the civil and financial administration are disconnected, their length of services and ranks in the colonial provinces receiving, as a rule, no recognition in the Peninsula.

"When these unjustifiable barriers within the same professions are leveled, the functionaries, both of the Peninsula and of the colonial provinces, will have within their reach a greater number of offices, the disqualifications due to incompatibility being removed.

* In Spain, as in France, Government services are professions, organized in ranks. Entrance into the service is by competitive examination; promotion, as a rule, by seniority. An officer if suspended retains his rank. There is a pension for long service.

and the Government will be able to select with greater freedom the employees that may be best fitted to fill the offices.

"Although the attainment of these objects will prove of very great advantage, it is surpassed in importance by a consideration which has primarily influenced your Majesty's Government; and that consideration is, that to establish the same reform in all the territory of Spain, to render its legislation uniform, to conciliate the conflicting interests of the various sections of the country, to assimilate its provinces, is to secure and strengthen the unity of the nation."

Article I. of this decree is as follows: "The personnels of the courts of justice, of the universities, institutes, special schools, normal schools and primary schools shall each constitute one profession, which shall be under similar regulations and shall serve without discrimination in the Peninsula and in the colonial provinces."

XXIII.

REMARKS.

THE AUTONOMIST PARTY.

Cuba Enjoys Privileges Denied to Other Spanish Provinces.

As has been shown, the present *régime* of the Spanish West Indies is the result of the tendency that has for a long time prevailed of assimilating them with Spain, turning them into Spanish provinces, with the institutions, rights and privileges of other provinces of Spain; and the legislation for them, which under the Constitution must either be special or must be the legislation of the Peninsula, with or without modification, far from lessening their privileges and local liberties, tends, on the contrary, to give them solid guarantees of prosperity, and exempts them from burdens imposed on all the other parts of the Spanish territory.

Thus the Cubans are exempt from military service, while the natives of the Peninsula serve for twelve* years in the army.

The Cuban exchequer is not liable for the debts of the national exchequer, whereas the latter guarantees the payment of the Cuban debt.

All the revenue collected from taxation in Cuba is used to satisfy the expenses of the administration of the island.

The Cuban treasury does not contribute to the expense of the Cortes, of the Appellate Courts, nor of the Superior Administrative

---

* Three years with the colors, the rest in the reserves.

Council and advisory boards, nor to the salaries of the diplomatic and consular representatives, all of which discharge their functions for the benefit of Cuba as well as for that of the rest of the nation.

The organization of the Cuban government may therefore be said to resemble the system of government of the British colonies rather than that of other European colonies. <small>*Similarity to the British Colonies.*</small>

All this has been stated by no one more eloquently than by the central committee of the Autonomist party in its address to the people of Cuba at the outbreak of the present revolt. The address bears the date April 4, 1895, and is subscribed with the names of the most eminent men of the party—men such as José Maria Galvez, Carlos Saladrigas, Juan Bautista Armenteros, Luis Armenteros Labrador, Manuel Rafael Angulo, Gonzalo Arostegui, José Buzon, José Maria Carbonell, José de Cardenas y Gassie, Raimundo Cabrera y Leopoldo Cansio, José A. de Cueto, Marques de Esteban, Rafael Fernandez de Castro, Carlos Fons y Sterling, José Fernandez Pellon, Antonio Gobin y Torres, Eliseo Giberga, Joaquin Güell y Rente, José Maria Garcia Montes, Manuel Francisco Lamar, Herminio C. Leiva, Ricardo del Monte, Federico Martinez Quintana, Rafael Montoro, José Rafael Montalvo, Antonio Mesa y Dominguez, Ramon Perez Trujillo, Pedro A. Perez, Leopoldo Sola, Emilio Terry, Diego Tamayo, Miguel Francisco Viondi, Francisco Zayas and Carlos de Zaldo. <small>*The Autonomist Party.*</small>

The address states that but for the outbreak of the revolt "the central committee would have performed the duty of addressing the country on the eve of the inauguration of a new *régime* in the adoption of which the representatives of the country had co-operated in an atmosphere of benevolence and concord they never before had felt in the metropolis, and to which they wished to bear true witness before their fellow citizens." <small>*Address of the Autonomists.*</small>

Such was the moment selected by the rebels to raise the standard of revolt against the mother country, which was intent upon the work of colonial reform. But the Autonomist party proved itself as firm in its principles as it was energetic in its protest against that which it described as "an anonymous and iniquitous raid, with a hurrah for every cause and a flag for every seditious act." And it adds: <small>*The Revolt Condemned by the Autonomist Party.*</small>

"The new *régime*, voted by the Cortes—which, if inaugurated in a time of peace and in the midst of the powerful current that had set in in favor of concord and progress through liberty, would have been prolific in immediate benefits and would have been a preparation to further advance—can never give such results if established amid the anxieties, the wrath, the resentments and the indignations of a civil war."

Progress Made Under Spanish Rule.

And further on, summing up "the important conquests made in the direction of colonial decentralization," it specifies the following:

"Abolition of slavery and of the apprenticeship to labor.

"Proclamation of the organic law of the state.*

"Freedom of the press, of peaceful assembly, of association, of education and of worship, to the same extent and with the same guarantees as in the mother country.

"Trial in open court.

"Civil marriage and registration thereof.

"All the modern civil and penal laws of the mother country.

"The abolition of differential duties and of export taxes.

"Expenditures reduced by 35 per cent. since the former war."

And it ends with these words :

"*The liberal party of 1878, which has seen in what manner the promises of the Zanjon Treaty have been performed and are being performed*, will not strike its flag, nor will it retreat before those who come to destroy the harvest of our toils, to turn us back from the path of peaceful progress, to lay waste the land, and to cloud the perspective of our future with the horrible spectres of misery, anarchy and barbarism ! "

The Autonomist Party Remains Loyal to Spain.

Such is the opinion of the Autonomist party of Cuba upon the true meaning of the revolt against Spanish domination. And what men can speak in this matter more authoritatively than the Cuban Autonomists ?

The form of government provided in the reform law proclaimed on March 23, 1895, is the limit of independence that can be granted to a province without absolutely breaking the bonds of union with the nation.

Reform Law of 1895.

That act provides for a council of administration consisting of thirty councillors, fifteen appointed by the Crown, the other fifteen elected by voters having the qualifications requisite to vote for provincial assemblymen. This council has the control of public works, posts and telegraphs, railways and navigation, agriculture, manufactures, trade, immigration and colonization, public instruction, charities, and the health department, and prepares and votes the appropriations for all these departments. It has a hearing upon the estimates of general taxation and expenditures of the island. These estimates, whether modified or not by the Supreme Government, shall always be laid before the Cortes. It has also a hearing upon the yearly general accounts of the exchequer ; upon the matters pertaining to the patronage of the Indies ; upon the decisions of the provincial governors that are appealed to the Governor-General ; and upon the suspension and removal of mayors and aldermen. The

---

* The Constitution was proclaimed in Cuba in 1875.

laws of municipalities and of provinces are amended to harmonize with the new act.

It is this law, so thoroughly in accord with the decentralization demanded by the Autonomist party, that has been greeted with bullets by the seditious element, who feared the effect of the liberal policy of the mother country upon their separatist plans.

XXIV.

REFORM LAW OF 1895.

LAW FOR THE REORGANIZATION OF THE GOVERNMENT AND CIVIL ADMINISTRATION OF THE ISLANDS OF CUBA AND PORTO RICO.

Alfonso XIII., by the grace of God and the Constitution, King of Spain, and, in his name and during his minority, the Queen Regent of the kingdom : To all whom these presents shall come, know ye that the Cortes have decreed and we sanctioned the following :

ARTICLE I. The system of government and the civil administration of the island of Cuba shall be readjusted on the following bases :

BASIS 1.

The laws of municipalities and of provinces, now in force in the island, are hereby amended to the extent necessary for the following ends:

The council of administration shall, upon the report of the provincial assemblies, decide all questions relating to the formation of municipalities, and to the determination of their boundaries.

Provincial Assemblies and Municipalities.

The law of provinces is hereby amended as to the matters placed by these bases within the powers of the council of administration.

The provincial assembly shall decide all questions pertaining to the organization of boards of aldermen, to their election, to the qualifications of the members and other similar questions.

Each board of aldermen shall elect one of its members as mayor. The Governor-General may remove a mayor and appoint a new mayor, but the new mayor must be a member of the board. In addition to their functions as executive officers of the boards of aldermen, the mayors shall be the representatives and delegates of the Governor-General.

Whenever the Governor-General shall stay the resolutions of a municipal corporation* the matter shall be laid before the criminal courts, if the stay be due to a misdemeanor committed by the corporation in connection with the resolutions, or laid before the provincial governor, upon the report of the provincial assembly, if the resolutions were stayed because they exceeded the powers of the board, or because they infringed the law.

The provincial governors may stay the resolutions of the municipal corporation, and censure, warn, fine or suspend the members of the corporations when they exceed the limits of their powers.

* See note page 66.

Previous to removing mayors or aldermen, in the cases provided by law, the Governor-General must give the council of administration a hearing upon the removal.

Every member of a municipal corporation who shall have presented, or voted in favor of, a resolution injurious to the rights of a citizen shall be under a liability, enforcible before the court having jurisdiction, to indemnify, or make restitution to, the injured party, the liability ceasing according to the rules of the Statute of Limitations.

Municipal Taxation.
Each board of aldermen shall, in matters defined as within the exclusive municipal powers, have full freedom of action, agreeably with the observance of the law, and with the respect due to the rights of citizens. In order that the boards of aldermen and the guilds* may fix the amount of the taxes to cover the expenses of the municipality and may determine their nature and their distribution, in accordance with the preferences of each municipality, the boards of aldermen and the guilds shall have all the powers necessary thereto, compatibly with the system of taxation of the state.

The provincial assemblies may review the resolutions of municipal corporations relating to the preparation or alteration of their estimates of revenues and expenditures, and, while respecting their discretionary powers, shall see that no appropriation which exceeds the assets be allowed, and that arrears of previous years and payments ordered by courts having jurisdiction have the preference. The Governor-General and the provincial governors shall in these matters have only the intervention necessary to insure the observance of the law and to prevent municipal taxation from impairing the sources of revenue of the state.

The annual accounts of each mayor, inclusive of revenues and expenditures, ordinary and extraordinary, shall be published in the municipality and audited and corrected by the provincial assembly, after hearing protests, and approved by the provincial governor if they do not exceed 100,000 pesetas,† and by the council of administration if they exceed that sum. The provincial assemblies and the council of administration shall determine what officials have incurred liabilities, except in the cases that come within the jurisdiction of the ordinary courts.

Appeals to the council of administration may be taken from the decisions of the provincial assemblies.

BASIS 2.

The Council.
The council of administration shall be organized as follows:

The Governor-General, or the acting Governor-General, shall be president of the council.

The Supreme Government shall appoint by royal decree fifteen of the councillors.

The council shall have a staff of secretaries, with the personnel necessary for the transaction of its affairs.

The office of councillor shall be honorary and gratuitous.

* For purposes of *taxation* the various trades are formed into guilds. Taxes on trades are apportioned among the guilds, whose officers fix the tax to be paid by each member according to the valuation of his business.

† $20,000.

Councillors Appointed by the Crown.

For appointment as councillor, the appointee must have resided in the island during the four years previous to appointment, and must have one of the following qualifications:

To be, or to have been, president of a chamber of commerce, of the Economic Society of Friends of the Country, or of the Sugar Planters' Association.

To be or to have been rector of the university, or dean of the corporation of lawyers of a provincial capital, for two years.

To have been for the four years previous to appointment one of the fifty principal taxpayers* of the island, paying taxes on real estate, on manufactures, on trade or on licenses to practice a profession.

To have been a senator of the kingdom or a representative to the Cortes, in two or more legislatures.

To have been two or more times president of a provincial assembly of the island; to have served for two or more terms of two years as member of the provincial executive committee;† or to have been a provincial assemblyman eight years.

To have been for two or more terms of two years mayor of a provincial capital.

To have been, until the proclamation of this act, member of the administrative council for two or more years.

The council may, whenever it shall deem it expedient, summon to its deliberations, through the Governor-General, any chief of department, but the latter shall not vote with the council.

Councillors Elected by the People.

To form the council fifteen additional councillors shall be elected by voters having the qualifications requisite to vote for provincial assemblymen.

The term of office shall be four years. The elections to fill vacated seats shall take place every two years, the provinces of Havana, Pinar del Rio and Puerto Principe voting at one election, and the provinces of Matanzas, Santa Clara and Santiago de Cuba voting at another.

The province of Havana shall elect four councillors; the province of Santiago de Cuba shall elect three; and each of the other provinces shall elect two.

All the councillors shall be elected at the same time: upon the establishment of this act, and after a total removal of the council. Two years after the establishment of this act, or after a total removal of the council the councillors from the first group of provinces above named shall vacate their seats, and their successors shall be elected.‡

In ordinary cases the election shall take place at the same time as the elections for provincial assemblymen, the votes for councillor and for assemblyman being cast together.

The council shall be the judge of the elections, returns and qualifications of the councillors-elect and of the qualifications of the

---

* See note p. 20.

† Each of the six provinces of Cuba—like every other Spanish province—has a provincial assembly. The assembly meets twice a year in sessions of about two weeks, and appoints from its members a provincial executive committee *comisión provincial*) to act during the intervals between the sessions.

‡ At the next election the councillors elected of the second group of provinces would vacate their seats.

councillors appointed by the Crown, and shall decide all questions concerning its own organization under the law.

BASIS 3.

Powers of the Council. The council of administration shall resolve whatever it may deem proper for the management in the whole island : of public works, posts and telegraphs, railways and navigation, agriculture, manufactures, trade, immigration and colonization, public instruction, charities and the health department, without prejudice of the supervision and of the powers inherent to the sovereignty of the nation, which are reserved by law to the Supreme Government.

Each year it shall prepare and approve the estimates with sufficient appropriations for all those departments. It shall exercise the functions that the laws of provinces and of municipalities and other special laws shall attribute to it. It shall correct, and in the proper cases approve, the accounts of its revenues and expenditures, which accounts shall be rendered every year by the general management of the local administration,* and shall determine the liabilities therein incurred by officials.

Revenues. The local revenues† shall consist of :

1. The proceeds of Crown lands and rents, and of the institutions whose financial management pertains to the council.

2. The surcharges which, within the limits fixed by law, the council may add to the taxes imposed by the state.

It shall be the duty of the Governor-General, as superior chief of the authorities of the island, to carry out the resolutions of the council.

For that purpose the general management of the local administration, as delegate of the Governor-General, shall attend to the departments included in the local estimates and shall keep the books thereof and shall be responsible for the non-fulfillment of the laws and of the legitimate resolutions of the council of administration.

Whenever the Governor-General may deem any resolution of the council contrary to the law or to the general interests of the nation, he shall stay its execution, and shall of his own motion take such measures as the public needs—which would otherwise be neglected—may require, immediately submitting the matter to the Minister of the Colonies.

If any resolution of the council unduly injures the rights of a citizen the councillors who shall have contributed with their votes to the passage of the resolution shall be liable, before the courts having jurisdiction, to indemnify or make restitution to the injured party.

Suspension of Members of Council. The Governor-General, after hearing the council of authorities,‡ may suspend the council of administration, or, without hearing the council of authorities, may suspend individual members of the coun-

* An office in charge of a superior official that under the Governor-General acts as the executive of the council of administration.

† Revenues of which the council of administration may dispose.

‡ See p. 55.

cil of administration, as long as a number of councillors sufficient to form a quorum remains:

1. When the council or any one of its members transgresses the limits of its legitimate powers, and impairs the authority of the Governor-General, or the judicial authority, or threatens to disturb the public peace.

2. For a misdemeanor.

In the first case the Governor-General shall immediately inform the Supreme Government of the suspension, so that the latter may either set it aside or, through a resolution adopted by the Council of Ministers within two months, decree the removal. If at the expiration of the two months the suspension has not been acted upon, it shall, as a matter of right, be deemed set aside.

In the second case, the matter shall come before the court having jurisdiction, which shall be the Supreme Court of Havana *in banc*, and its decision therein shall be final. In other cases the accused may appeal.

The council shall have a hearing: Advisory Powers of Council.

1. Upon the general estimates of expenditures and revenues of the island, which estimates, prepared by the finance department of the island, shall be submitted yearly, together with the changes suggested by the council, during the month of March, or earlier, to the Minister of the Colonies.

Although the Supreme Government may have varied the estimates before submitting them to the Cortes for appropriations to meet the expenses of the departments and the general obligations of the state, it shall always submit with them, for purposes of information, the changes suggested by the council.

2. Upon the general accounts, which the finance department of the island must without fail submit annually within the six months following the end of the fiscal year, and which shall include the revenues collected and the expenditures liquidated.

3. Upon the matters pertaining to the patronage* of the Indies.

4. Upon the decisions of provincial governors which shall come on appeal before the Governor-General.

5. Upon the removals or suspensions of mayors and aldermen.

6. Upon other matters of a general nature.

The Governor-General may demand of the council the reports he may desire.

The council shall meet in ordinary sessions at stated intervals, and in extraordinary session whenever the Governor-General may summon it.

BASIS 4.

The Governor-General shall be the representative of the National Government in the island of Cuba. He shall as vice-royal patron exercise the powers inherent to the patronage of the Indies. He Powers and Duties of the Governor-General.

---

* In England when lords of manors first built and endowed churches on their lands they had the right of nominating clergymen (provided they were canonically qualified) to officiate in them. This right is the "patronage" (*jus patronatus*). The Bulls of Alexander VI. in 1493 and of Julius II. in 1508 granted the Crown of Spain the patronage of the Indies (new world). It includes not only the right of presentation to the churches and monasteries built and endowed by the Crown, but other rights so extensive that the author speaks of the kings of Spain as the "born delegates of the Holy See and apostolic vicar-generals in the Indies."

shall be the commander-in-chief of the army and the navy stationed on the island. He shall be the delegate of the Ministers of the Colonies, of State, of War and of the Navy. All the other authorities of the island shall be his subordinates. He shall be appointed and removed by the President of the Council of Ministers, with the assent of the council.

In addition to the other functions which pertain to him by law or by special delegation of the Government it shall be his duty :

To proclaim, execute and cause to be executed, on the island, the laws, decrees, treaties, international conventions and other mandates that emanate from the legislature.

To proclaim, execute and cause to be executed the decrees, royal orders, and other mandates that emanate from the executive and which the Ministers, whose delegate he is, may communicate to him.

To suspend the proclamation and execution of resolutions of his Majesty's Government when, in his judgment, such resolutions might prove injurious to the general interests of the nation or to the special interests of the island, informing the Minister concerned of the suspension, and of the reasons therefor, in the speediest manner possible.

To superintend and inspect all the departments of the public service.

To communicate directly upon foreign affairs with the representatives, diplomatic agents and consuls of Spain in the Americas.

To suspend, after consultation with the council of authorities, the execution of a sentence of death, whenever the gravity of the circumstances may require it, and the urgency of the case be such that there is no opportunity to apply to his Majesty for pardon.

To suspend, after consultation with the same council, and on his own responsibility, whenever extraordinary circumstances prevent previous communication with the Supreme Government, the constitutional rights expressed in Articles IV., V., VI. and IX., and Sections 1, 2 and 3 of Article XIII. of the Constitution of the State, and to apply the Riot Act.

It shall also be the duty of the Governor-General as head of the civil administration :

To keep each department of the administration within the limits of its powers.

To devise the general rules necessary for the execution of the laws and regulations, submitting them to the Minister of the Colonies.

To conform strictly to the regulations and orders devised by the Supreme Government for the due execution of the laws.

To determine the penal institutions in which sentences are to be served, to order the incarceration therein of convicts, and to designate the jail liberties when the courts order confinement therein.

To suspend any public official whose appointment pertains to the Supreme Government, giving the Government immediate notice of the suspension, with the reasons therefor, and to fill *pro tempore* the vacancy in accordance with the regulations now in force.

To act as intermediary between the Ministers whose delegate he is and all the authorities of the island.

Council of Authorities.

The council of authorities shall consist of the following members : the Bishop of Havana, or the Reverend the Archbishop of Santiago de Cuba, if the latter be present; the commander of the naval station; the military governor; the presiding justice of the Supreme Court of Havana; the attorney-general; the head of the department of finances, and the director of local administration.

The resolutions of this council shall be drawn up in duplicate and one of the copies shall be sent to the Minister of the Colonies. They are not binding upon the Governor-General. All his acts must be upon his own responsibility.

The Governor-General shall not surrender his office nor absent himself from the island without the express order of the Supreme Government.

In case of vacancy, absence or inability, the military governor shall be his substitute, and in default of the latter the commander of the naval station, until the Supreme Government appoints a *pro tempore* governor-general.

The criminal part of the Supreme Court at Madrid shall have the sole jurisdiction over the Governor-General for infractions of the Penal Code. Charges of maladministration against the Governor-General shall be brought before the Council of Ministers.

The Governor-General shall not amend nor revoke his own decisions when they: have been confirmed by the Supreme Government; or have vested rights; or have served as the basis of a judgment of a court, or of the adjudication of a mixed juridical-administrative tribunal; or when he bases his decision upon the limitations of his powers.

BASIS 5.

The civil and financial administration of the island, under the supervision of the Governor-General, shall be organized in accordance with the following rules:

Civil and Financial Administration.

The Governor-General, with his staff of secretaries, which shall be under the direction of a chief of department, shall attend directly to matters of government, the patronage of the Indies, conflicts of jurisdiction, public peace, foreign affairs, jails, penitentiaries, statistics, personnel of the departments, communication between all the authorities of the island and the Supreme Government, and all the other matters that are unassigned.

The finance department, which shall be under the charge of a superior chief of department, shall attend to the whole management of the finances; it shall keep the books, and audit and submit the accounts of the estimates of the state on the island.

The provincial administrative sections shall be under the direct control of the finance department, without prejudice of the supervision that the Governor-General may delegate in fixed cases to the provincial governor.

The general management of local administration, under the charge of a superior chief of administration, shall attend to the departments that shall be supported with the appropriations made by the council of administration; it shall keep the books, and audit and submit the annual accounts of the estimates of the council and of the municipalities, and shall enforce the resolutions of the council of administration.

The personnel of the offices and the methods for the transaction of affairs shall be adapted to the object of obtaining the greatest simplicity in the transaction of affairs and in fixing official responsibility.

The rules of law shall determine the cases in which a right is vested through the decision of a superior official in a matter that, in accordance with this basis, falls within his jurisdiction, so that an action before the mixed juridical-administrative tribunal may lie.

Nevertheless the injured party may at any time bring a complaint before the Governor-General in matters which concern the finance department and the general management of local administration, and also before the Minister of the Colonies in any matter that concerns the administration or the government of the island; but the complaint shall not interrupt the administrative process, nor the legal procedure, nor the course of the action before the mixed juridical-administrative tribunal.

The Governor-General and the Minister of the Colonies, when using their powers of supervision, either on their own initiative or owing to a complaint, shall refrain from interrupting the ordinary course of affairs, as long as there be no necessity of taking measures to remedy or prevent irreparable damage, before the final decision of the competent authority.

ART. II.* The system of government and the civil administration of the island of Porto Rico shall be readjusted upon the following bases:

BASIS 1.

Reforms for the Island of Porto Rico.

The law of municipalities, now in force in the island, is hereby amended to the extent necessary for the following ends:

Questions relating to the formation of municipalities and of municipal corporations, combinations of several municipalities into one, determination of the boundaries of municipalities, elections, qualifications of voters, and other analogous questions shall be settled, without appeal, by the provincial assembly.

Each board of aldermen shall elect one of its members as mayor. The Governor-General may remove the mayor and appoint a new mayor, but the new mayor must be a member of the board.

Whenever the Governor-General shall stay the resolutions of municipal corporations the matter shall be laid before the criminal courts, if the stay be due to a misdemeanor committed by the corporation in connection with the resolutions, or laid before the provincial governor, upon the report of the provincial assembly, if the resolutions were stayed because they infringed the law.

The delegates of the Governor-General may stay the resolutions of municipal corporations, and censure, warn, fine or suspend the members of the corporations when they exceed the limits of their powers.

Previous to removing, in the cases provided by law, mayors or aldermen, the Governor-General must give the council of administration a hearing upon the removal.

Every member of a municipal corporation who shall have presented, or voted in favor of, a resolution injurious to the rights of a citizen shall be under a liability, enforcible before the court having

---

*Art. II. of this act refers exclusively to Porto Rico. Art. III. refers both to Cuba and to Porto Rico.

jurisdiction, to indemnify, or make restitution to, the injured party, the liability ceasing according to the rules of the Statute of Limitations.

Each board of aldermen shall, in matters defined as within the exclusive municipal powers, have full freedom of action, agreeably with the observance of the law and with the respect due to the rights of citizens.

In order that the boards of aldermen and the guilds may fix the amount of the taxes to cover the expenses of the municipalities and may determine their nature and their distribution, in accordance with the preferences of each municipality, the boards of aldermen and the guilds shall have all the powers necessary thereto, compatibly with the system of taxation of the state.* Municipal Taxation. (P. R.)

The provincial assembly may review the resolutions of municipal corporations relating to the preparation or alteration of their estimates of revenues and expenditures, and, while respecting their discretionary powers, shall see that no appropriation which exceeds the assets be allowed, and that arrears of previous years and payments ordered by courts having jurisdiction have the preference. The Governor-General and the provincial governors shall, in those matters, have only the intervention necessary to insure the observance of the law and to prevent municipal taxation from impairing the sources of revenue of the state.

The annual accounts of each mayor, inclusive of revenues and expenditures, ordinary and extraordinary, shall be published in the municipality and audited and corrected by the provincial committee, after hearing the proper officials upon the corrections, and shall be allowed or disallowed, without appeal, by the provincial assembly, which shall determine, also without appeal, what officials have incurred liabilities, except in the cases that come within the jurisdiction of the ordinary courts.

Art. CXVIII. of the present law of municipalities of Porto Rico is hereby amended.

BASIS 2.

The law of provinces now in force in the island of Porto Rico shall be amended to the following ends:

For the purposes of Articles LXXXII. and LXXXIV., and in accordance with Article LXXXIX. of the Constitution, the whole island shall continue to form one province, divided into two regions.

The provincial assembly shall consist of twelve assemblymen, six from each region. The term of office shall be four years. The election to fill vacated seats shall take place every two years, the region of San Juan voting at one election and the region of Ponce at another. All the assemblymen shall be elected together: upon the establishment of this law; and after a total dissolution of the assembly. Two years after the establishment of this law, or after a total dissolution of the assembly, the assemblymen of the first named region shall vacate their seats, and their successors shall be elected. A majority of the members of the assembly shall constitute a quorum. Provincial Assembly. (P. R.)

The provincial assembly shall elect its president; it shall be the judge of the elections, returns and qualifications of the assembly-

---

* See note page 51.

men-elect, and shall decide all questions referring to its own organization under the law. The Supreme Court of the island shall have exclusive jurisdiction over appeals from the decision of the provincial assembly in these questions.

The Governor-General, after hearing the council of authorities, may suspend the provincial assembly, or without hearing the council of authorities may of his own motion decree the suspension of individual members, as long as a number of assemblymen sufficient to form a quorum remains :

1. When the provincial assembly or one of its members transgresses the limits of its legitimate powers, and impairs the authority of the Governor-General, or of the judicial authority, or threatens to disturb the public peace.

2. For a misdemeanor.

In the first case the Governor-General shall immediately inform the Supreme Government of the suspension, so that the latter may either set it aside or, through a resolution adopted by the Council of Ministers within two months, counted from the date of departure of the first direct mail for the Peninsula, decree the removal. If at the expiration of the two months the suspension has not been acted upon, it shall, as a matter of right, be deemed set aside. In the second case the matter shall come before the courts having jurisdiction and their decision shall be final, both as to the suspension and as to liabilities incurred by officials.

Powers of the Provincial Assembly. (P. R.) The provincial assembly shall resolve, in accordance with the laws and regulations, whatever it may deem proper for the management in the whole island, of public works, posts and telegraphs, railways and navigation, agriculture, manufactures, trade, immigration and colonization, public instruction, charities and the health department, without prejudice of the supervision and of the powers inherent to the sovereignty of the nation, which the laws reserve to the Supreme Government. Each year it shall prepare and approve the estimates, with sufficient appropriations for those departments, and shall exercise the functions that the law of municipalities and other special laws shall attribute to it. It shall audit and, in the proper cases, approve the accounts of the provincial revenues and expenditures, which accounts shall be rendered every year by the section of local administration, and shall determine the liabilities therein incurred by officials.

Revenues. (P. R.) The revenues for its appropriations shall consist : first, of the proceeds of the lands and rents that are the property of the province or of the institutions whose management pertains to the provincial assembly ; second, of the surcharges which the law may authorize upon the taxes of the state, which are collected by the finance department of the island ; and third, of the contributions it may demand from the municipalities, the contributions being apportioned among the municipalities in proportion to their revenues.

It shall be the duty of the Governor-General, as supreme chief of the authorities of the island, to carry out the resolutions of the council. For that purpose, as delegate of the Governor-General, the section of local administration of the general government of the island shall attend to all the departments included in the provincial estimates, the accounts of which it shall keep, and shall be responsible for non-observance of the law and of the resolutions of the assembly.

Whenever the Governor-General may deem any resolution of the provincial assembly contrary to the laws or to the general interests of the nation, he shall stay its execution, and shall of his own motion take such temporary measures as the public needs—which would otherwise be neglected—may require, immediately submitting, together with the report of the council of administration therein, the matter to the Minister of the Colonies.

If any resolution of the provincial assembly unduly injures the rights of a citizen, the assemblymen who shall have contributed with their votes to the passage of the resolution shall be liable, before the court having jurisdiction, to indemnify, or to make restitution to, the injured party.

There shall be in the regions of San Juan and of Ponce delegates of the Governor-General, with the rank, pay and powers proper to further the transaction of administrative affairs and the discharge of the duties of the Governor-General.

Basis 3.

The council of administration of the island of Porto Rico shall be organized and shall discharge its functions in the manner hereinafter expressed.

The Council of Administration. (P. R.)

The following shall be president and councillors *ex officio:*

The Governor-General.
The Reverend the Bishop of Porto Rico.
The military governor.
The commander of the naval station.
The presiding justice of the Supreme Court.
The district attorney.
The lieutenant-colonel of the volunteers of the capital.

The provincial assemblymen of the region in which the next biennial election shall take place.

The Supreme Government shall appoint by royal decree six more councillors, two of whom shall have the legal qualifications,* the rank and the salary of chief of department of the first class,* and shall prepare the reports necessary for the deliberations of the council.

The council shall have a staff of secretaries, with the personnel necessary for the transaction of its affairs.

The office of all the councillors, except the reporters,† shall be honorary and gratuitous.

Previous service on the island for one year shall be an indispensable qualification for appointment as reporter in the council of administration.

For appointment as councillor, with the exception of the reporters, the appointee must have one of the following qualifications:

To be or to have been president of a chamber of commerce, of the Economic Society of Friends of the Country, or of the Association of Agriculturists.

* See note below.
†*Ponentes*, the two councillors mentioned above, who must be chiefs of department.

To be or to have been director of the Institute of San Juan, or dean of the corporation of lawyers of San Juan de Puerto Rico, for two years.

To have been for the four years previous to appointment one of the fifty principal taxpayers of the island, paying taxes on real estate, or one of the fifty principal taxpayers paying taxes on a license to practice a profession, on manufactures, or on trade.

To have been a senator or representative to the Cortes in two or more legislatures.

To have been elected two or more times president of the provincial assembly, or two years mayor of San Juan de Puerto Rico.

The council may, whenever it may deem it expedient, summon to its deliberations, through the Governor-General, the chiefs of department, to hear them, without giving them a vote.

The functions of the council shall be purely advisory. A majority shall constitute a quorum. It may appoint committees from among its members to inquire into the matters upon which it may have to report.

It shall have a hearing:

Advisory Powers of Council. (P. R.)

1. Upon the general estimates of expenditures and revenues of the island, which estimates, prepared by the finance department of the island, shall be submitted annually, together with the changes suggested by the council, within the month of March or earlier, to the Minister of the Colonies. Although the Supreme Government may have varied the estimates before submitting them to the Cortes for appropriations to meet the expenses of the departments and the general expenses of the state, it shall always submit with them, for purposes of information, the changes suggested by the council of administration.

2. Upon the general accounts, which the finance department of the island must, without fail, present annually within the six months following the end of the fiscal year and which shall include the revenues collected and expenditures liquidated.

3. Upon the matters pertaining to the patronage of the Indies.

4. Upon the resolutions of the provincial assembly which occasion the intervention of the Governor-General, as provided in Basis 2.

5. Upon the petitions for legislative reforms that emanate from the provincial assembly before their submission to the Supreme Government.

6. Upon the removals and suspensions of mayors or aldermen.

7. Upon all other matters that the laws may determine.

The Governor-General may demand of the council all the reports he may desire.

BASIS 4.

Powers and Duties of the Governor-General. (P. R.)

The Governor-General shall be the representative of the National Government in the island of Porto Rico. He shall, as vice-royal patron, exercise the powers inherent to the patronage of the Indies. He shall be the commander-in-chief of the army and the navy stationed on the island. He shall be the delegate of the Ministers of the Colonies, of State, of War and of the Navy. All the other authorities of the island shall be his subordinates. He shall be appointed and removed by the President of the Council of Ministers with the assent of the council and upon the proposition of the Minister of the Colonies.

In addition to the other functions which pertain to him by law or by special delegation of the Government, it shall be his duty:

To proclaim, execute, and cause to be executed, on the island, the laws, decrees, treaties, international conventions and other mandates that emanate from the legislative power.

To proclaim, execute and cause to be executed the decrees, royal orders and other mandates that emanate from the executive, and which the Ministers, whose delegate he is, may communicate to him.

To suspend the proclamation and execution of resolutions of his Majesty's Government when, in his judgment, such resolutions might prove injurious to the general interests of the nation or to the special interests of the island, informing the Minister concerned of the suspension and of the reasons therefor in the speediest manner possible.

To superintend and inspect all the departments of the public service.

To communicate directly upon foreign affairs with the representatives, diplomatic agents and consuls of Spain in the Americas.

To suspend, after consulting with the council of authorities, the execution of a sentence of death, whenever the gravity of the circumstances may require it, and the urgency of the case be such that there is no opportunity to apply to his Majesty for pardon.

To suspend, after consultation with the same council, and on his own responsibility, whenever extraordinary circumstances prevent previous communication with the Supreme Government, the constitutional rights expressed in Articles I., V., VI. and IX., and Sections 1, 2 and 3, **Art. XIII.**, of the Constitution of the state, and to apply the Riot Act.

It shall also be the duty of the Governor-General, as head of the civil administration:

Other Executive Duties. (P. R.)

To devise the general rules necessary for the execution of the laws and regulations, submitting them to the Minister of the Colonies.

To conform strictly to the regulations and orders devised by the Supreme Government for the due execution of the laws.

To determine the penal institutions in which sentences are to be served, to order the incarceration therein of convicts and to designate the jail liberties when the courts order confinement therein.

To suspend any public official whose appointment pertains to the Supreme Government, giving the Supreme Government immediate notice of the suspension, with the reasons therefor, and to fill *pro tempore* the vacancy, in accordance with the regulations now in force.

To act as intermediary between the Ministers, whose delegate he is, and all the authorities of the island.

The council of authorities shall consist of the following members: The Reverend the Bishop of San Juan de Porto Rico, the military governor, the commander of the naval station, the presiding justice of the Supreme Court of San Juan, the attorney-general, the head of the Department of Finance, and the chief of the section of local administration.

Council of Authorities. (P. R.)

The resolutions of this council shall be drawn up in duplicate and one of the copies shall be sent to the Minister of the Colonies. They are not binding upon the Governor-General. All his acts must be upon his own responsibility.

The Governor-General shall not surrender his office, nor absent himself from the island, without the express order of the Supreme Government. In case of vacancy, absence or inability, the military governor shall be his substitute, and in default of the latter the commander of the naval station, until the Supreme Government appoints a *pro tempore* Governor-General.

The criminal part of the Supreme Court at Madrid shall have the sole jurisdiction over the Governor-General for infractions of the Penal Code. The charges against the Governor-General for maladministration shall be brought before the Council of Ministers.

The Governor-General shall not amend nor revoke his own decisions when : they have been confirmed by the Supreme Government ; or have vested rights ; or have served as the basis of a judgment of a court or of the adjudication of a mixed juridical-administrative tribunal ; or when he bases his decision upon the limitations of his powers.

A decision of the Governor-General, of a ministerial nature, or in a matter lying within his discretion, or when it assumes a reglementary character, may be revoked or modified by the Supreme Government, whenever the latter may judge such decision contrary to the laws or general regulations, or injurious to the government and good administration of the island.

Civil and Financial Administration. (P. R.)
The civil and financial administration of the island, under the supervision of the Governor-General, shall be organized in accordance with the following rules :

The Governor-General, with his staff of secretaries, which shall be under the direction of a chief of department, shall attend directly to matters of government, patronage of the Indies, conflicts of jurisdiction, public peace, foreign affairs, jails, penitentiaries, statistics of personnel of the departments, communications between the authorities of the island and the Supreme Government and all other matters that are unassigned.

The finance department, which shall be under the charge of a superior chief of department, shall attend to the whole management of the finances ; it shall keep the books and audit and submit the accounts of the estimates of the state in the island. The administrative sections of the two regions shall be under the direct control of the finance department, without prejudice of the supervision that the Governor-General may delegate in fixed cases to the regional governors.

The section of local administration, under the charge of a chief of department, shall attend to the departments that shall be supported with the appropriations made by the provincial assembly ; it shall keep the books, and audit and submit the annual accounts of the provincial estimates, and of the municipalities, and shall enforce all the resolutions of the provincial assembly.

Official Responsibility. (P. R.)
The personnel of the offices and the methods for the transaction of affairs shall be adapted to the object of obtaining the greatest simplicity in transacting affairs and in fixing official responsibility.

The rules of law shall determine the cases in which a right is vested through the decision of a superior official in a matter that in accordance with this basis falls within his jurisdiction, so that an action before the mixed juridical-administrative tribunal may lie.

Nevertheless the injured party may at any time bring a complaint before the Governor-General in matters which concern the finance department and the management of administration, and also before the Minister of the Colonies in any matter that concerns the administration or the government of the island; but the complaint shall not interrupt the administrative process, nor the legal procedure, nor the course of an action before the mixed juridical-administrative tribunal.

The Governor-General and the Minister of the Colonies, when using their powers of supervision, either on their own initiative or owing to a complaint, shall refrain from interrupting the ordinary course of affairs, as long as there be no necessity of taking measures to remedy or prevent irreparable damage, before the final decision of the competent authority.

ART. III. The system of election and the division of the provinces into districts for the provincial elections shall be modified by the Government, in order to enable minorities in both Cuba and Porto Rico to have representation in the municipalities and in the provincial assemblies, and in Cuba in the council of administration of Cuba; and in order to apply to the election of aldermen, provincial assemblymen, and councillors of administration—in so far as the qualifications of voters and the annual formation and rectification of the registration lists are concerned—the provisions of the royal decree of December 27, 1892, upon the reform of the electoral law for the election of representatives to the Cortes, Articles XIV., XV. and XVI. of the said royal decree shall be extended to all classes of elections. *Provincial Elections.*

For all electoral purposes the taxes imposed by the council of administration in Cuba, and by the provincial assembly in Porto Rico, by virtue of the new powers granted to them by this act, shall be computed as if imposed by the state.

ADDITIONAL ARTICLE.

The Government shall render the Cortes an account of the use it makes of the powers hereby granted to it.

TRANSITIONAL PROVISIONS.

1. The councillors of administration elected in the island of Cuba upon the proclamation of this act shall stay in office until the first election for provincial assemblymen that happens after two years have passed since the first election of the council.

2. The rectification, according to the methods that shall be established under Art. III of this act, of the registration lists for the election of aldermen and of provincial assemblymen in both Cuba and Porto Rico, and of councillors of administration in Cuba, shall commence from the time of the proclamation of this act.

The Minister of the Colonies shall ordain, by royal decree, the necessary measures, and shall fix the time for the various operations of the rectification, so that it may be finished before any election take place to establish the council of administration in Cuba or to fill the seats of members of municipal corporations whose terms have expired.

The election for the latter purpose shall under no circumstances be postponed, except in the case of the boards of aldermen,* which, in this present year, and if the Supreme Government deem it necessary, may be postponed until the first fortnight of next June.

In subsequent years the rectification shall take place in the manner provided by the royal decree of December 27, 1892, referred to in Art. III. of this act.

Therefore:

We order all the courts, justices, chiefs, governors and other authorities, civil, military and ecclesiastical, of whatsoever class or dignity, to keep, and cause to be kept, fulfill and execute this act in all its parts.

Given in the Palace, March 15, 1895.

I, THE QUEEN REGENT.

The Minister of the Colonies,

BUENAVENTURA ABARZUZA.

XXV.

CONCLUSION.

Rebels Cannot Specify Grievances. At the termination of the former rebellion the only condition imposed upon the capitulants was the acknowledgment of the sovereignty of Spain.

The best evidence of the faithfulness with which the successive Spanish Ministers have performed the promises of the Zanjon capitulation, and given Cuba a stable and progressive government during the seventeen years of unbroken peace in the island, is the fact that the very men who to-day are breaking their solemn treaty pledges have confined themselves to generalities, being unable to state specific grievances.

Spain has granted Cubans political rights to the same extent as they are possessed by the other Spanish citizens, without impediment or restriction whatsoever; it has conceded to them civil liberties, guaranteed by the Constitution; and has given them economic liberties under the protection of which the wealth and the commerce of the island, privileged by the fertility of its soil, have enormously increased.

Spain has made concessions that are more than legitimate. She has surrendered the local government of the Spanish West Indies to the initiative of their sons, and given them admission to all the ranks of the administration of the state.

To Cuba the Spanish flag means security to life and property, and a steady advance in civilization and prosperity. Spain cannot

---
* Municipal corporations in Cuba, as in the Peninsula, have a board of aldermen (*ayuntamiento*) and a municipal council (*junta municipal*).

deprive her loyal Cuban children of the benefits of her rule and abandon them into the hands of a turbulent minority, untrained in the art of government. No, Spain cannot grudge, nor will she grudge, the sacrifices of men and money that may be rendered necessary by the unjustifiable revolt of the reckless men who are in arms against their mother country, "confining themselves to an irregular system of hostilities, carried on by small and illy armed bands of men, roaming, without concentration, through the woods and the sparsely populated regions of the island, attacking from ambush convoys and small bands of troops, burning plantations and the estates of those not sympathizing with them." *

<small>Gen Grant's Opinion of the Insurgents.</small>

No wonder that at the repetition of so lamentable a spectacle the Prime Minister of Spain uses the following unanswerable argument :

"We cannot admit that the slightest ground exists for the recognition of the belligerency of the Cuban insurgents, whose so-called President and the members of his executive council are nomads, like the rebel bands, ever on the move."

April, 1896.

---

* President Grant's message of June, 1870.

APPENDIX.

In 1850 the foreign trade of Cuba amounted to $50,000,000, and in 1878 was nearly double that amount, the exports alone reaching over $60,000,000, while for the year 1892 we have the following figures:

Importations,	$69,444,287
Exportations,	101,014,266
Total,	$170,458,553

This carrying trade may be divided as follows:

In Spanish vessels,	$63,702,557
In foreign vessels,	106,755,996
Total,	$170,458,553

The total value of trade between Cuba and the United States for 1892 was as follows:

Exports to the United States,	$89,327,000
Imports from the United States,	20,185,000
Total,	$109,512,000

In 1894 the value of merchandise imported from the United States into Cuba was $33,617,000.

Taking the bulk of the foreign trade in connection with the population of Cuba, reducing it to a proportion per capita and comparing it with the similar rate obtained for the Spanish-American republics in 1892, we have the following diagram:

CUBA.

Population, 1,600,000. $106 per inhabitant.   Foreign trade, $170,000,000.

URUGUAY.

Population, 700,000. $83 per inhabitant.   Foreign trade, $61,000,000.

COSTA RICA.

Population, 243,000. $45 per inhabitant.   Foreign trade, $18,000,000.

CHILE.

Population, 2,800,000. $42 per inhabitant.   Foreign trade, $130,000,000.

BRAZIL.

Population, 14,000,000. $40 per inhabitant.   Foreign trade, contos de reis 587,000,000.

HAYTI.

Population, 572,000. $35 per inhabitant.   Foreign trade, $20,000,000.

PORTO RICO.

Population, 800,000. $27 per inhabitant.   Foreign trade, $33,000,000.

VENEZUELA.

Population, 2,300,000. $19.50 per inhabitant.   Foreign trade, $36,000,000.

ARGENTINA.

Population, 4,000,000. $15 per inhabitant.   Foreign trade, $242,000,000.
                                                                                        (Paper money)

As for the other Spanish-American republics, such as Mexico, Guatemala, Nicaragua, Salvador, Colombia, Peru, Bolivia, &c., the proportion of the foreign trade to the population does not amount to $10 per capita.

No better proof can be adduced of the activity and prosperity attained by the island of Cuba under Spanish rule than the above comparison.

The following official statistics show the increase in crops, commerce, railroads and population:

Sugar Crop.

Years.	Tons.
1878,	530,598
1879,	680,700
1880,	547,089
1881,	483,945
1882,	500,357
1883,	484,976
1884,	560,934
1885,	630,414
1886,	705,403
1887,	610,171
1888,	630,311
1889,	526,439
1890,	645,894
1891,	819,760
1892,	976,789
1893,	815,894
1894,	1,018,028

Tobacco Crop.

Years.	Value.
1879,	$17,560,000
1894,	20,829,000

Shipping, 1894.

	Ships.	Tons.
Ships arrived,	3,748	4,358,555
Ships sailed,	3,713	4,050,488
Totals,	7.461	8,409,044

Railroads.

		Miles.
Concessions from 1834 to 1879—		
Public,	1,002	
Private,	61	
		1,063
Concessions from 1879 to 1896—		
Public,	179	
Private,	273	
		452
Total miles,		1,515

Population.

	1857.	1879.	1887.
White,	579,490	984,632	1,102,889
Colored,	444,510	482,211	528,798
Totals,	1,024,000	1,466,843	1,631,687

TAXES.

TAXES ON AGRICULTURAL PRODUCTS.

Rate of Taxation.*

1867,	Ten per cent. (on net profit).
1868–1878,	Rose to 35 per cent.
1880–1881,	{ On sugar and tobacco, 10 per cent. { Other products, 16 per cent.
1882–1883,	{ On sugar and tobacco, 2 per cent { Other products, 8 per cent.
1883–1884 to date,	ALL PRODUCTS, 2 PER CENT.

EXPORT TAXES.

Until 1880–1881 a tax on all agricultural products of 1 per cent. and a surcharge† of 10 per cent.

1881—The act of June 5, 1880, reduced the tax by 15 per cent.

1883—The surcharge reduced to 5 per cent.

1886—The act of August 5, 1886, increased the reduction of 15 per cent. (of 1881) to 20 per cent.

TAX ON SUGAR PRODUCTION.

1892—The act of June 30, 1892, imposes a tax of 10 cents upon every 100 kilograms (220 pounds) of centrifugal sugar, and of 5 cents upon every 100 kilograms of muscovado and molasses.

1893—The act of August 6, 1893, reduced the tax on sugars by 50 per cent. and abolished the tax on molasses.

1895—The act of February 20, 1895, abolished the tax.

---

* This is on the *net profits* of cultivation. A certain per cent. of the market price of the crop is deducted for expenses. For some years 60 per cent. of the market price (estimated) was the deduction for the expenses of the cultivation of coffee. Thus in 1883, when the tax was 2 per cent., if the value of the crop were $1,000 the cultivator would pay a tax of 2 per cent. on $400; that is to say, $8.

† The surcharge is on the amount of the tax. Thus, if the value of the article be $1,000 the tax would be $10 and the surcharge $1, making a total tax of $11.

EXPENDITURES.

From 1879 to 1895.

Estimate of Expenditure Subsequent to the Zanjon Treaty.

1878-79,	$46,594,688
1880-81,	44,035,850
1882-83,	35,860,249
1883-84,	34,170,880
1885-86,	31,169,653
1886-87,	25,959,734
1888-89,	25,596,441
1890-91,	24,446,810
1891-92,	25,214,645
1892-93,	23,074,594
1893-94,	26,037,394
1894-95,	The same

COMPARATIVE TAXATION.

During the last seven years the revenue of Cuba has been estimated at $25,000,000, which gives a per capita taxation among the 1,600,000 inhabitants of $15.30. Here is a comparative table of the taxation per capita, embracing several Spanish-American countries :

Countries.	Total Revenue.	Rate per Capita.
Chile,	$65,000,000	$23
Brazil,	208,000,000	22
Uruguay, .	14,000,000	20
Costa Rica,	4,900,000	19
Argentina.	67,000,000	16
Hayti.	9,000,000	16
Cuba,	25,000,000	**15**
Porto Rico,	5,000,000	8

www.ingramcontent.com/pod-product-compliance
Lightning Source LLC
Chambersburg PA
CBHW020252090426
42735CB00010B/1887